OCCASIONAL CONTRIBUTIONS FROM THE MUSEUM OF ANTHROPOLOGY OF THE UNIVERSITY OF MICHIGAN
NO. 14

CULTURE AND AGRICULTURE

An Anthropological Study of a Corn Belt County

BY

HORACE MINER

ANN ARBOR
UNIVERSITY OF MICHIGAN PRESS
1949

ISBN (print): 978-1-949098-50-1
ISBN (ebook): 978-1-951538-49-1

Browse all of our books at
sites.lsa.umich.edu/archaeology-books.

Order our books from the University of Michigan
Press at www.press.umich.edu.

For permissions, questions, or manuscript queries,
contact Museum publications by email at umma-pubs@umich.edu or visit the Museum website at
lsa.umich.edu/ummaa.

PREFACE

THE following study germinated in a series of conferences on cultural anthropology held during May, 1939, in the office of Undersecretary M. L. Wilson, of the United States Department of Agriculture. It was the desire of the undersecretary to ascertain if the functional analyses of society and the concept of culture utilized by certain sociologists and anthropologists could be fruitfully applied to problems of the Department. The conclusion of the conference was that the cultural approach might give the Department new insight into farm life and its problems. To pursue this end, Dr. Carl C. Taylor, head of the Division of Farm Population and Rural Welfare, was authorized to start a series of studies of characteristic farm areas.

This first study was almost exploratory in its initial design. The actual purposes and emphases were evolved as the study progressed. This process was assisted by conferences with Doctors C. C. Taylor, John Provinse, Charles P. Loomis, Ralph Danhof, all then of the Department of Agriculture, and with Professors Robert Redfield and Lloyd Warner, of the University of Chicago, who acted in an advisory capacity.

I am, likewise, indebted for courteous assistance in this study to Professor Ray Wakeley, of Iowa State College; Mr. Walter Eyre, county agent of Hardin County; and Mr. Herbert G. Folken, acting Bureau of Agricultural Economics representative in Iowa.

The field period consisted of less than four months' residence and study in Hardin County, beginning August 1 and ending December 15, 1939, with about three weeks out of the county for conferences and other Department of Agriculture activity. The report on the study was submitted to the Department of Agriculture in 1940 in practically the same form as it appears here.

The attempt to make a community study bear upon the implications of a controversial national governmental policy was a tactical error, considering the fact that the study was made for a division of a government bureau involved in the policy. This report immediately stirred up controversy over the advisability of publication. The head of the division ultimately decided to publish the study, but it was "lost" in the shifts occurring during his absence in South America. Subsequent studies were more carefully oriented and edited before publication in the series of *Rural Life Studies*. In spite of precautions, a political furore of such magnitude developed over one study that the division has been forbidden to publish any more cultural surveys. Under these circumstances the head of the division has kindly consented to release the material of this report for publication. The point of view expressed in the monograph is obviously mine and not that of the Department of Agriculture.

CONTENTS

I
PROBLEM AND METHOD

UPON the initiation of this study, the problem proposed by the Department of Agriculture was no more specifically defined than "the application of the cultural approach to the study of farm life in the corn belt." Determination of the unit of investigation and, even more important, the emphases of the study were the preliminary part of the work.

The first decision made was to choose between a study designed to isolate the typical elements of a culture area, and an intensive study of the culture of a community chosen from a certain area. In spite of the apparent logical necessity of first distinguishing a culture area, this line of investigation was not followed. This decision was made for several reasons: (1) The spatial definition of a culture area and the delimitation of typical traits of that area consist of the recognition of traits present in various contiguous communities—in this sense the study of the community must precede that of the culture area, (2) in the study of a community, the culture can be treated as a whole and the interrelationship of its parts analyzed, which is the essence of the functional approach in which the Department of Agriculture was interested, and (3) a type of culture area study was already available which could be made the basis of selection of a sample community.

The study undertaken, therefore, was an attempt to add to our knowledge of the totality of a type of American culture of which corn-livestock agricultural economy is one phase. The method was the analysis of a selected community of that general economic type. This does not imply that the particular community studied is representative or typical of all rural communities based on this sort of economy. An attempt was made to choose a community which would possess as many of the features common to corn-belt farmers as possible. In selecting the community for study, cultural islands, unique developments of unusual geographic features, farm areas on an economic base marginal to the corn-livestock type, and excessive urban influence were avoided.

From what we already know of American rural culture, no socially independent local unit is discernible. The farm is linked to the town and city in the broader cultural framework. The emphasis of this study being farm life, it was decided to consider the behavior of farmers in the light of their local cultural context. Thus, influences from without, entering through regular institutionalized channels, are as much a part of the picture as local tradition, but return influences on government and business are beyond the scope of this study. Similarly, the social organization of the rural town was not data for the study, except inasmuch as it affected the farmer on the farm.

The anthropologist's functional approach to culture consists in part of a field method and in part of a descriptive framework for the synthesis of his findings. These techniques are so oriented as to show the functional interrelationships between the various aspects of the culture—the frame of reference basic to the whole approach.

The attempt to describe the totality of a culture may, in fairness, have the criticism leveled at it that it dabbles in all aspects of culture but becomes master of none. The answer to such criticism is that by describing, even in a meager fashion, the interrelation of major aspects of culture, a clearer concept of the actual social whole can be gained than by writing numerous unrelated special treatises, each with its own frame of reference and school of thought. This does not deny that the greater the thoroughness which can be achieved in the over-all picture, the better it will be.

Anthropologists have largely confined their studies to simple, small, and homogeneous cultures. The complexity, numerical greatness, and heterogeneity of any part of the corn belt immediately set limitations on the thoroughness of any study which could be made in the time available. This was partly offset by the availability of special studies and documentary evidence. It seemed desirable, however, to select certain aspects of the culture for special attention, so far as this could be accomplished without abandoning the basic approach. Inasmuch as the study was being made for the Department of Agriculture, I decided to point the emphasis of the study toward those aspects of corn-belt culture which were involved in the relations between the farmers and the action agencies of the Department of Agriculture. This emphasis was expressed as the hypothesis that "the nature of a culture sets limits on the type of change which can be affected in it." Basic to the testing of this hypothesis, it was necessary to draw some broad picture of the culture and its values. In depicting the general social fabric, well-documented technological traits of the culture, such as details of material culture or principles of scientific farming, were eliminated as being beyond the scope of this study.

The selection of a unit of study was also affected by the limiting factors already mentioned as well as the categories of extant statistics. It was decided that a county was the largest unit which it was feasible to study and which would contain most aspects of rural life. It was on this basis that the selection below was made. After some time in the field, emphasis was shifted to the trade area of the county seat, a more natural unit, and one roughly half the size of the county.

The selection of a representative county of the corn belt was based upon a wide variety of data. The basic delimitation of the general area for investigation was drawn from a study of A. R. Mangus,[1] which delimits farm culture areas and subareas primarily on the basis of types of farming. Refinements of these areas are based on county statistics on the rural-farm plane of living index (1930), population fertility ratio (1930), and percentage of farm tenancy (1935), in addition to other socio-economic data.

Mangus' "Upper Midwest" cultural region is a refinement of the corn belt. The Upper Midwest region is divided into subareas. The marginal subareas represent cultural blends with adjacent regions, so search for a locale for this study was confined to the large central subarea. This focus on a central sub-

[1] A. R. Mangus, *Cultural Regions within the Rural-Farm Population* (Washington: Div. Soc. Res., W.P.A., 1938).

area was in accord with the general anthropological concept of central location of "typical" groups in a culture area. Mangus selected the most typical counties of the subarea by taking those whose indices fall within 5 per cent of those for the median county of the subarea. On this basis he designates ten counties as the most typical of the subarea; seven of these are in Iowa, two in Nebraska, and one in Illinois. Again, because of the apparent central position and typical nature of Iowa, further tentative consideration was restricted to these seven Iowa counties.

The census was consulted to find the typical period of settlement of the area and more recent population trends. After checking the seven counties against this information, one was rejected because of its atypical rapid growth during the decade 1920–30. This county also had a larger proportion of the population gainfully employed outside of agriculture. These variations, due to the presence of the city of Ames in the county, were felt to make that area undesirable for study.

The population make-up of all seven counties was consulted for the period after the greatest growth (1890) and both foreign born and their children were recorded for 1930. The dominant stocks represented were found, and one county was ruled out as a possibility, because of a large number of one stock which was unrepresented elsewhere among the typical counties. A third county was dropped from consideration as it had an exceedingly high proportion of immigrants and their children. An examination of religious affiliation by counties bore out the picture obtained from immigration statistics.

The seven counties were checked to discover if they had the soils prevalent in the corn belt. Mining in one county made it an unsuitable choice. One county was very close to Des Moines and was therefore eliminated.

The two counties which had none of the special disadvantages noted above were about equidistant from surrounding large cities. These two counties were checked against distribution maps of all crops and livestock, both in the state and over the corn belt. Neither county had exceptional features.

Between these two counties, Montgomery and Hardin, the latter seemed preferable because of its greater soil diversity, including Carrington soil, which is present both in Illinois and in Iowa. It was also more centrally located with respect to the total area. Final selection of Hardin County was not made until the area had been visited and the county agent and members of the sociology faculty at Iowa State College, who were familiar with the area, had been consulted.

After some time spent in the county, my attention was called to another study in which Hardin County had been selected as

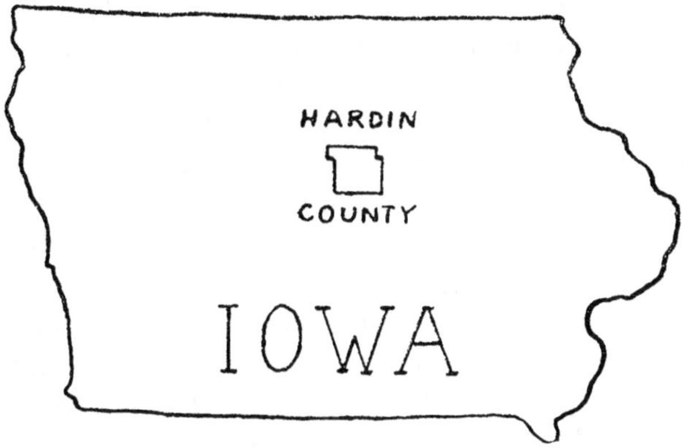

FIG. 1. Hardin County, Iowa.

characteristic of rural Iowa (almost all of which falls in the corn belt). The bases of this selection are included here:

The aim in choosing an area for the investigation was to get a county that was as nearly representative of rural Iowa as possible; including persons living in the open country (rural farm), villages (preponderantly rural non-farm) and towns (urban). Accordingly, 13 counties which appeared to meet this criterion were considered further. The counties . . . were ranked from one to thirteen according to each of the following criteria: (1) number of aged persons in the county; (2) percent of aged persons to the total population of the county; (3) percent of aged persons receiving old age assistance . . . ; (4) farm income for the county as a whole; (5) number of foreign born persons in the county; (6) percent total foreign born aged persons were of the total aged persons; (7) the countries from which the largest and the next largest number of foreign persons came. Hardin County was found to be more nearly representative than the other counties considered.[2]

The only unusual features in Hardin County are a small state park and a state reform school, neither of which affects the culture of the county to any extent. In retrospect, this county still seems an ideal choice. There was possibly a greater intellectual element in this area than elsewhere, which makes the county more progressive, but the distortion is slight as the element itself is found throughout the corn belt.

The method of investigation consisted largely of living in the area and observing the culture by means of personal informal contacts with the farmers and townfolk. With my family I kept house in the county seat during all of the period except the last week, during which I boarded with a farm family in the country, participating in their daily routine. Local style clothes were worn, a local car license obtained. In short, everything possible was done to fit into the cultural picture. My presence was explained as that of a college teacher studying farm life, a perfectly clear position to these persons who were well acquainted with the agricultural college at Ames. In order to get perfect frankness with respect to government action programs, no affiliation with the Department of Agriculture was alluded to, except with the county agent, who was asked not to mention it.

First contacts with farmers were as free from the sponsorship of others, who might prejudice the informants, as possible. Thus, instead of going around with the county agent or a welfare worker, I made contacts with farmers in the barn lot, field, town, and at church. I attended public meetings of all kinds, and private occasions as the opportunity arose. Direct questioning had to be utilized, but leading questions were avoided and, whenever possible, the conversation was simply guided into desired channels. In addition, various documentary accounts

[2] Lawrence S. Bee, "The Incidence of Selected Social Factors upon Old Age Dependency." Unpublished master's thesis, Iowa State College, 1937.

and studies of the county were consulted and some original statistical work was done from county records. A soil map and particularly a plat book were indispensable in gaining familiarity with the farmers and their farms. Collateral reading of the novels of Iowa farm life, such as Stong's *State Fair* and Suckow's *The Folks*, was suggestive and illuminating.

II

EARLY AND RECENT HISTORY[1]

THE westward moving wave of settlers spilling across the Mississippi and flooding over the wild western prairies, reached central Iowa in the middle of the past century.[2] Contrary to present popular belief and the explicit statements of the hardy pioneers themselves, the spirit which motivated this surge to the West was not the desire "to found a home" in the traditional sense, but rather a yearning to "get ahead," to better one's situation. Security was left, not sought. The drive for progress at the expense of the safe and friendly traditional ways continues to the present.

In this same desire for advance we see the reason why willingness to do hard work was a cardinal virtue. Settlers were not trying to make a simple living, but the best one they could manage out of the variables of opportunity, effort, and method. The opportunity was the new soil, the effort was their own labor, and the method was open to the continuous improvement of farm machinery and technique.

[1] This section does not purport to present an historical continuum, nor is it simply to contrast the old and the new. Its purpose is to give something of the old roots of the culture in order to contribute to the understanding of the present social framework. The more recent background gives insight into cultural detail which will be important in understanding the culture's reaction to more recent social innovations. Sources include the local newspaper files, minute books, court and other county records, interviews with old citizens and two books: *History of Hardin County* (Springfield, Ill., 1883) and Frank T. Clampitt, *Some Incidents in My Life* (Ann Arbor, Mich., 1935). Herbert Quick's historical novels give a fine picture of the period of settlement in the immediate vicinity.

[2] In 1830 nowhere in Iowa did the population density reach two persons a square mile. By 1860 the density of all of the eastern half of the state was more than six persons to the square mile and only the northwest corner remained under two. The same settlement waves can be seen in Illinois, starting some twenty years earlier, although the corn-belt area lagged ten years behind. The change in population density of the entire corn-belt area of Illinois and Iowa from below two to over six persons a square mile was accomplished in sixty years.

The first settler on the soils of Hardin was a Kentuckian who built his cabin by the Iowa River in 1849. The next year several other families moved into the same general vicinity and soon two more settlements were started a few miles up the river. The following spring there was a migration of Quakers from North Carolina, who formed a settlement of forty persons on a tributary of the Iowa. Other settlers came largely from the long-established agricultural areas of the East and Midwest. In 1870, the largest number of Iowa residents born elsewhere came from Ohio; and then in order followed Pennsylvania, Indiana, and New York. By the turn of the century, there was a marked shift westward in point of origin, such that, in order of numbers, Illinois was first, followed by Ohio and Indiana. Illinois has continued to be the greatest source of Iowans outside of Iowa itself, a significant fact when considering the cultural homogeneity of the corn belt.[3] Study of a random selection of old settlers from one of the first townships to be settled in Hardin County shows that many of those born in the East settled for short periods in Illinois before continuing to Iowa, again illustrating their desire to search out greater opportunities, not just "a home."[4]

Possibly the most striking aspect of this early settlement period is the rapidity with which these pioneers duplicated the formally organized social environment which they had left. They wanted to progress materially, but in a world like that in which they had grown up. So, while they were still poverty-stricken, even by their own standards, they busied themselves re-creating the life they knew. Only five years after the first settler came to the region, the county had two established

[3] C. J. Galpin and T. B. Manny, *Interstate Migrations* (Washington: Dept. Agric., 1934), p. 39.

[4] In a group of twenty-six first settlers of Eldora Township, state and country of birth were as follows: Ohio, six; North Carolina, three; Pennsylvania, three; Kentucky, three; Ireland, three; Indiana, two; and one each from Tennessee, New York, New Jersey, Massachusetts, Scotland, and England. However, the states the people left on coming to Iowa are Illinois, fifteen; Ohio, three; Indiana, three; Pennsylvania, three; and North Carolina, two.

churches and two schools, county officials were selected and a court of law was operative, and a doctor had been practicing for three years. The next two years saw the formation of an agricultural society and the establishment of a newspaper, a sawmill, and a store. Life began to take on its old context—the frontier was giving way before the progressive drive of the settlers.

This social progress did not imply, however, any comparable material gain. Residences were log cabins or sod-covered "three-faced camps," earthen-floored, and exposed on one side. The people were practically self-sustaining with the small amount of equipment and stock they brought with them. They had trekked halfway across the continent in linchpin wagons, the women and children walking and driving the cattle all the way. Few even saw a railroad on the whole trip, and there was not a mile of rail in Iowa. The roads were only beaten trails clinging to high ground as they meandered across the prairies. The settlements themselves were invariably made along the wooded streams as here was lumber, shelter, water, and the source of necessary game. In fact, it was doubted at the time that the prairie would ever be settled, as the fertility of land was judged by the stand of timber on it.

Life was not only primitive, it was also precarious. The people were never really threatened by Indians, but the panic caused by a rumored raid in the early years shows some mental unrest attributable to the proximity of the "red man." Aside from snake bite and frequent serious accidents, the greatest danger was that of disease. Typhoid epidemics were serious, and malaria ("the shakes") was prevalent, supposedly due to the fact that this was a "new country of rank soil."

A rank soil it was, too, with ponds, marshes, and swamps abounding, yet the highland clearings were fertile. The sod was broken with "bar-share" walking plows, with the farmer's daughter almost invariably at the reins. The women also dropped seed corn in spaded holes and covered the seeds with a hoe. Men sowed the wheat broadcast in fields tilled with plow and wooden-toothed harrow, and then the seeds were covered by means of a brush drag. The mature grain was cut by hand with sickle or cradle. Three cradles cut ten acres a day and one binder kept pace with each cradle. It was hard work, but the harvest gang had a hilarious time. After curing in the shock, the wheat was usually threshed by trampling horses, although there was some flailing. Winnowing was rarely by wind action, but by mechanical fanning mills. After all was done, it was at least a full day's haul of a fifty-bushel load to the nearest grinding mill. If there was a surplus, it might be sold at the mill for about thirty cents a bushel. It was a life full of hard work with small financial remuneration.

No one was rich, and there was a great deal of lending of surplus meat or grain to less fortunate neighbors, with no thought of profit. Frontier simplicity made even a man with a spring seat on his wagon seem "stuck up." From this openhandedness and social equality under conditions of insecurity for all, the growth of means and a feeling of assured economy contributed to the individuation of the farm family and emphasis on the profit motive.

This family independence in the place of interdependence has only recently reached anything like completeness, and the drive for independence has been in part responsible for the mechanization of the farm. Neighborhood butchery bees and threshing crews continued as long as they were of practical advantage to the participant families. The community and neighborhood were units of recreation for a longer period. The dancing of reels, sets and jigs, shivarees for newlyweds, church picnics, quilting bees, and the like furnished the needed relaxation and amusement. Much of the same enjoyment was attendant upon neighborhood co-operative activities of a more economic nature.

As the county developed and prospered, not only were legitimate enterprises attracted to the area, but gamblers, cattle rustlers, swindlers, and undesirable elements of all sorts came in as well. The county and its new towns conformed rather well to the present popular conception of the "mushroom" towns of the West of that period. The rumor in 1853 of gold in the county, based on the presence of unprofitable quantities, brought in two or three thousand persons in a single summer. Farmers turned quickly to the fastest method of getting rich.

Court records during the first score of years reveal the strength of community sentiment against lawlessness, the danger from itinerants, the frequency of sex irregularities, and something of family difficulties. The first case tried in the county was one for divorce, in which the man brought suit and gained custody of the children. During the next term of court four of the thirty-seven cases were for divorce. On a change of venue, four men were charged with assault with intent to murder for tar and feathering a squatter. They were found guilty and fined twenty dollars apiece. Suits against liquor sellers, forgers of land titles, horse thieves, the murderer of a bullying drunkard, a timber stealer are all recorded. Other cases reveal a forced marriage and the death of a girl from abortion, rape and murder by an itinerant worker, adultery charges preferred by an irate husband against a French doctor. Not on the books are the vigilante activity of the Hardin County Mutual Protection Society against horse thieves and the murder of other horse stealers by a mob which broke into the county jail. Never brought to dock were the defalcating county auditor and a cracksman who looted the county safe of $13,000.

Regional and personal struggles for dominance, pursued within the limits of the law, also marked the early period. No sooner had a commission settled on Eldora for the county seat, than other settlements, through local pride and an eye to business, clamored for a change. Three years after the creation of the county seat, Steamboat Rock, a community just north of Eldora, lost a popular election to change the county seat. The next year Berlin, after submitting a petition signed by half the active voters, lost out in the final vote in a similar attempt. The following year Point Pleasant won, by a margin of nineteen votes, a popular vote to change the county seat. The transfer of county records was restrained by an injunction until after a recanvas of votes, during which a spurious poll book from

Pleasant Township was thrown out, giving Eldora the majority again. Litigation over this election continued unfruitfully for the next ten years, even reaching the state supreme court, the plaintiff claiming partiality on the part of the judge involved in the election recount, for the judge owned a great deal of property in Eldora.

Even more important to the financial progress of the county and of Eldora was the obtaining of railroad connection, as the

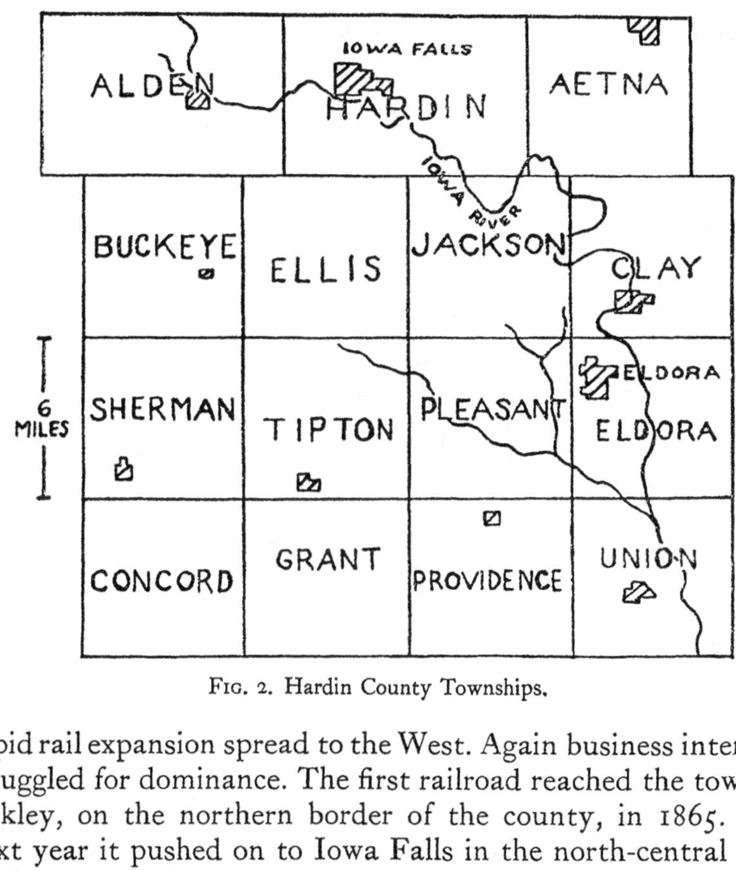

FIG. 2. Hardin County Townships.

rapid rail expansion spread to the West. Again business interests struggled for dominance. The first railroad reached the town of Ackley, on the northern border of the county, in 1865. The next year it pushed on to Iowa Falls in the north-central part of the county. It is significant that the *Sentinel*, a newspaper which had been printed in Eldora for almost ten years, moved to Iowa Falls in 1865 because of "the little hope we once had of railroad communication between this place (Eldora) and the outer world has fled. . . ." The editor "saw the handwriting," for Iowa Falls has continued its railway superiority over Eldora, to the commercial embarrassment of the latter town.

Eldora secured a rail connection to Ackley in 1868 by means of claiming to possess valuable coal deposits. But the mines never developed into a major enterprise and have long been abandoned. By 1881 the rail network in the county was practically complete. Iowa Falls secured three rail connections; Eldora two, on roads which were not major runs.[5] Comment in the newspapers of the time gives the feeling about railroads rather well:

> The purchase by the C. & N.W.R.R. company of the road known as the "Toledo Plug" virtually secures to Eldora an eastern outlet. It is no secret that parties have been in Eldora within a few days looking the ground over with a view to extending the "Plug" to this city.[6]

The neighboring county paper commented:

> The Eldora people are getting terribly worked up on the question of the extension of the Toledo plug. Every time they pass through Gifford they listen anxiously for the engine. . . . The Eldora people's idea now is to . . . build a road from a point east of Gifford to Iowa Falls via Eldora.[7]

The railroads facilitated settlement. Between 1860 and 1880 foreign immigrants came to the county in large numbers. They took up prairie land, as the more valuable river lands were already occupied. Today a third of the population are European immigrants and their immediate descendants. The largest group is of German extraction, the next most common being Norwegian. These two stocks account for three-quarters of the

[5] Iowa Falls was on the Dubuque and Sioux City Railroad, the Chicago and Northwestern, and the Burlington and Cedar Rapids; now, respectively, Illinois Central, the Chicago and Northwestern, and the Chicago, Rock Island, and Pacific. Eldora was on the Central Iowa Railroad, now the Minneapolis and St. Louis, and the Chicago and Northwestern.

[6] *Eldora Herald*, Oct. 8, 1879.

[7] *Grundy Center Republican*, Dec., 1879.

entire group, and the origin of the remainder is scattered among twenty-odd other countries, particularly other Scandinavian countries and England. There was a marked tendency for Germans and Scandinavians to settle in concentrations based on cultural identity.[8] However, they are represented in all townships to some extent. Whereas the immigrants in these areas of concentration once tried to maintain cultural isolation from the Yankee settlers,[9] the second generation has been assimilated to a great extent. The distinctiveness of the Yankee[10] and of the immigrant population elements is still an important part of local culture.

Tax assessment lists of farm land show some interesting shifts of value in the score of years preceding 1882. With the successful "breaking of the prairie," the older settlements along the river decreased markedly in value relative to the rest of the county, with the exception of the townships in which Eldora and Iowa Falls were growing towns.[11] Land values on the whole had almost doubled, and the best land was that newly settled by Norwegians in the western part of the county. This shift toward

[8] The Scandinavian center is in Concord Township and extends into the neighboring areas, outside the county as well as within. One German concentration in Aetna and Clay townships constitutes the fringe of a German concentration in neighboring Grundy County. Another German center occupies Tipton, Grant, Sherman, and Buckeye, which form another block of contiguous townships in Hardin County.

[9] In Grundy County the German community had such solidarity that it refused to allow a Yankee to buy into their midst in spite of the fact that he had married a German girl.

[10] The term "Yankee" is used throughout this report to designate the old American settlers and their descendants in distinction to recent immigrants to the United States and their children. The latter are Americans but not of the "Yankee" cultural heritage.

[11] With the exclusion of the four townships formed during the period of comparison, Union, where the first settlement was made, slipped from first to sixth place in relative land value. Clay, through which the river also runs, went from fourth to ninth. Ellis values failed to increase, moving her relative position from first to tenth. (Union and Ellis were tied for first in 1861). This drop is probably due to speculation in the township in the early days as its settlement was not early.

higher values in the western part of the county, rather than in the longer settled but less fertile east, has continued until today. As roads were built, the advantage of being close to the larger towns declined and fertility alone determined farm value.

While the economic philosophy of the farmers was based on doing everything in their power to produce more crops and animals, with a rather general feeling of impotence with respect to the price structure, the businessmen of the larger rural towns felt their welfare depended upon luring as many enterprises into the community as possible. The businessmen promoted and fought over the location of the county seat, the newspaper, the railroad, the mill, the hotel, and so on. The source of income was rarely considered. Two items appearing almost simultaneously in the newspaper in 1889 illustrate the businessman's lack of concern over farm conditions and what he did consider important:

> Money is scarce with the farmers. They don't like to sell oats at fifteen cents and corn at eighteen cents.[12]
>
> Our people have rallied to the support of the new hotel with commendable liberality and up to date $9,400 has been subscribed.[13]

In the trading contact between town and farm, the farmer's gain was the townsman's loss, and this feeling of competition and opposition, fostered by the more rapid assimilation of urban ways in the town, still underlies the thinking of both farmer and businessman.

Not everyone prospered as the towns grew and the production of the farms rose. By 1875 the county found it necessary to purchase a poor farm, and it immediately had twenty-two inmates. By the end of the century, in addition to the poor farm, public aid, in the form of coal, goods, and medical assistance, was extended to twenty paupers.[14] As corn was at twenty-seven cents and hogs at thirty-five, this unusual demand on the

[12] *Eldora Herald*, Dec., 1889.

[13] *Ibid.*, Nov. 29, 1889.

[14] Five cases were purely medical, three others were widows, and only four received any dry goods.

county caused the newspaper to suggest publication of the pauper list and to query:

> Do they work? Are they able to work? Have they come to regard the feeding from public charity as an honorable and satisfactory thing to do? . . . if the matter is taken out 'in meeting' (they) will come to see and feel the pressure of public opinion and will make an effort to keep off the list.[15]

The residents of Hardin County respected other basic values in addition to the economic ones. One of these was the great worth felt to be inherent in education. This desire to provide schooling for the children is well illustrated by the early start and rapid development of the county schools. The first school dates from the creation of the county in 1853. By 1871 there were ninety-two school houses, largely frame, and 159 teachers including fifty-five men. The average monthly salary was forty-three dollars for men and thirty-three dollars for women. Almost 70 per cent of the five to twenty year age group was enrolled, although attendance amounted to only about half of that. Ten years later there were thirty-eight more schools, one thousand more students, three teachers less, and the teacher's pay had been cut eight dollars a month. The farmers believed in education as evidenced by the schools and the enrollment. The adequacy of instruction was of lesser importance, an attitude which still persists. The teachers were inadequately trained, being largely high-school graduates who taught long enough to lay aside a little money and then got married. A school superintendent in his report in 1881 commented on the situation:

> There is entirely too much crude practice required to fit these immature aspirants for instructors, and by the time they are somewhat fitted, the mass of them leave the work, to be replaced by another ephemeral class, and so the protoplastic condition is continued.

The training for teachers consisted largely of courses in various academies and "subscription schools." The best known academy was that at New Providence. The tuition was nominal,

[15] *Eldora Herald*, Oct. 11, 1898.

and students boarded or kept rooms for themselves. Many grade-school graduates were prepared there, in the course of ten weeks of training, to pass their examinations for teacher's certificates. One such boy, who passed his examinations at the age of fourteen and was allowed to start teaching at sixteen, later became governor of Illinois.

Just as the fact of "having an education" was more important than the kind of training one had, so also being religious was more important than belonging to any particular denomination. This was more true of the Yankee stocks, for the German and Norwegian immigrants, who later settled in large numbers in the county, clung to their Lutheran and Evangelical dogmas. The Methodist, Christian, and Presbyterian churches and Friends Meeting were the earlier established denominations, followed by the Baptists and Congregationalists. Where several denominations were represented in a single town, each began to take on a distinctive class position. Church quarrels and schisms in congregations followed these status lines. In the country the tendency was for farmers to attend the closest church, irrespective of what their former denominational affiliations had been. Many who did not attend church at all were still strong believers in Christian ethics and the fundamental teachings and divine inspiration of the Bible.

This section of the "Bible Belt" was also strongly in favor of temperance, if not prohibition. This did not mean any unanimity of opinion, for the immigrants from abroad, as well as some of the rougher elements, liked alcoholic drinks. As early as 1855 the state submitted to vote the question of allowing the sale of hard liquor. Hardin voted prohibition 153 to ninety. In 1870 state law permitted each county to regulate its own sale of wine, ale, and beer. Hardin went dry 908 to 584. Newspaper editorials of the day ascribed 94 per cent of the crime of the state and 55 per cent of its insanity to alcohol.

The medical practitioner, like the teacher, held the confidence and respect of the citizens of Hardin. Actually, this confidence was not always well placed. Some of the first "doctors" were utterly untrained. Homeopathic and "eclectic" physicians continued in popularity even after the establishment of excellently trained doctors of medicine in the county. The settlements apparently attracted two types of medical practitioners—well-educated young men looking for a community to which to minister, and charlatans looking for prey. It was a doctor in the town of Ackley who is supposed to have been responsible for the archaeological hoax of the Cardiff Giant, which made headlines all over the country. While doctors held a respected position and were called with readiness in case of illness, childbirth, or accident, the merits of the practitioner were never greatly questioned. An anecdote of the early period illustrates this very well. A farmer came miles to see the doctor about an ailment, only to find it necessary to wait for the doctor's return. In conversation with the doctor's hired man, the farmer discovered that the servant had held his position for many years. Thereupon the farmer asked the servant for treatment, "as you certainly must have learned a lot in that time."

The period of development of the county cannot be left without reference to the rapid sequence of changes which occurred in farm technique. Wheat was the crop which paid for the opening of the new lands. Implements connected with the cultivation of this crop were the first to show improvement. The seeder and drill had superseded hand sowing by 1870. Reapers developed so rapidly that each became obsolete in six or seven years.[16] In the early seventies farmers used the Buckeye Dropper which cut the grain and dumped it in untied bundles. Three men followed the machine tying the bundles and moving them out of the path of the reaper. This machine was soon replaced by a self-rake McCormick, which was drawn by a four-horse team and was followed by six men to do the binding. Transient labor came into the state from as far away as North Carolina, following the reapers and earning three to four dollars a day. This large reaper, which disappeared by 1885, to be followed by the Marsh harvester, was the forerunner of the self-

[16] The authority for this section on machines and their trade names is Clampitt (*op. cit.*). All of the competing machines are not given here, only enough of the well-known ones to picture the trend.

binder. It necessitated hand binding and was slower than the McCormick, but it was "easier and on the whole less expensive." To offset its lack of speed, it was run far into the night. Machinery was bought to increase production and profit, not to lighten labor. Simplifying a task meant being able to do more, so the farmers continued to purchase new machinery, through the various types of self-binders down to the harvesters of today which do the threshing as well.

During the seventies marshy farms were beginning to be tilled by their owners and barbed-wire fencing became very popular. The county agricultural society was reorganized and held the first fair since that held ten years previously. The growing number of buildings to shelter grain and stock[17] was pointed to with pride and the decreased interest in artificial groves was being decried. Hog and corn raising were on the increase.[18] Corn culture involved "checking" a field and then planting it with a horse-drawn hand dropper. Corn picking came late in the season and was arduous labor. In extreme instances, it was even harvested at sixteen degrees below zero, almost up to Christmas. Farmers picked so late in the day that "it got so dark you could not see to quit." Just as corn picking was dreaded, it also became the medium through which rural youth could express its manhood in the tangible form of the number of bushels picked a day, a hundred bushels being common.

The interests, attitudes, and activities of the early period find excellent summation in the make-up of the newspaper of the period. The paper served three major functions: It was a commercial venture for owner and advertisers; it was the formalization of gossip in the expanded community, passing on news and rumors, taking sides, playing politics, criticizing and censoring; and it also served as a source of literature, providing fiction and poetry for the readers. For example, in the issue of October

[17] Although buildings to shelter machinery and equipment were reported, they never became fixed in the culture patterns. The lack of care of machinery is a striking feature today.

[18] County crops, 1874: 38,454 acres of wheat (497,251 bushels); 41,304 acres of corn (1,379,960 bushels); 10,982 acres of oats (356,945 bushels).

1, 1879, of the *Eldora Herald*, the advertising gives much insight into the period. The largest advertisements on the front page are for a railroad and for a furnishing and undertaking establishment, "Undertaking and Picture Framing a Specialty." In addition are smaller notices, as "Opium and Morphine Habit Cured," "Marriage Guide and Rubber Goods," "Seminal Pastile to Cure Impotency," "Private Medical Advisor for ills of self-abuse and excess." Land agents and attorneys, a homeopathic physician, hotels, a carriage shop, a harness shop, and a jeweler also had small advertisements.

Advertising on the second page of the paper was one-sixth national in character, consisting of eight different patent medicines to cure everything from consumption to impotency. The local advertisements were for groceries, dry goods, shoes, jewelry, books, monuments, pumps, town lots, wagons, harness, livery, tailoring, banking, photography, hair dressing, and various services. The final page of the paper sold western land, the newspapers of large cities, wagon scales, sewing machines, organs, song books, and patent medicines, including Mexican Mustang Linament, "A Balm for Every Wound of Man and Beast."

The first page of the paper included true stories from other papers, such as "Almost Buried Alive," the story of the origin of coal; President Hayes's speech, stories about, and verbal attacks on, the Democrats of the South, and a column of jokes. The next sheet reported on local politics and that in other states, an accident as the result of a runaway team, and a railroad scandal and lawsuit. There was also a literary section with extracts from *Scribner's*, *St. Nicholas*, *Peterson's Magazine*, *Frank Leslie's Sunday Magazine*, and an encyclopaedia.

The general content of the local news varied from that of today in the presence of items involving horses—loss of a beast from colic, a kicking horse breaking someone's arm, or the establishment of a new smithy. The increased yield of present crops is notable by contrast. Twenty bushels of wheat and seventy-five bushels of corn to the acre were cause for comment in 1879. At the local market, wheat was bringing sixty-five to eighty-two cents and corn shelled or on the ear twenty cents. Eggs were seven cents a dozen and butter ten cents a pound.

"Visiting Notices" indicate remarkable population mobility. People were leaving Hardin to journey to Minnesota on a fishing trip and to Kansas and the larger towns in Iowa, such as Waterloo and Muscatine. Friends and relatives from Nebraska, Wisconsin, Illinois, and New York were coming to visit in Eldora. Local human interest stories reported a fire, a ball game, weddings, births, illness, accidents, deaths, political meetings, new houses, a lawn sociable, and a five-legged chicken. Local news was under the headings of various towns and townships[19] in the southern part of the county and Iowa Falls in the north. Lodge and church items were numerous. Several columns of "Sabbath" headings were on the last page along with the foreign news review.

Local antagonisms, fostered by ethnocentric pride as well as business competition, found frequent physical expression through fist fights. The newspaper was also the organ for the expression of belief in local superiority. The *Marshall Times* accused Eldora of making war on beer sellers and arresting, fining, and imprisoning them illegally to which the *Eldora Herald* responded:

> We suggest to the *Times* . . . that it give a little of its unutilized space to the cleaning out of the brothels, dram shops and gambling hells that infest Marshall. You will have your hands full, neighbor, if you regenerate and purify your own cesspool of abominations.[20]

The *Herald* jumped with apparent joy on the sermon of a Baptist minister of Iowa Falls, in which he said there were drunken carousals every evening, that a party of young men engaged a room where a woman outdid "Little Egypt" in her dancing, that drug stores were saloons, and that there were clubs where young men and boys met to gamble and drink.[21]

Two weeks later, after the Iowa Falls paper claimed "a great

[19] Eldora, Union, Providence, Steamboat Rock, Grant, Tipton.

[20] *Eldora Herald*, Oct. 8, 1879.

[21] *Ibid.*, Aug. 30, 1898.

wrong" had been done, the *Herald* printed a retraction of its statement that Iowa Falls hotels were houses of ill fame by quoting the pastor's correction: "What I said was that there was one place in this city in which you can pay for your board and prostitution at the same time."

Bickering of this sort functioned largely to express antagonisms between competing communities. It was rarely intended to clean up the situation, although the Eldora papers did fight the temperance battle long and hard. But even the ministers were not in position to express from the pulpit more criticism than the congregation wanted to hear. The newspaper eulogy of a pastor of particular merit praised him for "his scholarly attainments" and his teaching of the "gospel of pure religion," which meant sermons which allowed the congregation to make their own applications of the lesson. The *Herald* even found newsworthy:

> A new preacher told a Cedar Rapids congregation that in all his wide experience in western wickedness, he had nowhere observed so much moral depravity covered with alleged respectability.

The paper commented:

> There will be an epidemic of backsliding unless the new preacher discourses upon agreeable subjects.[22]

The present short term of pastorate in this area represents a continuation of this early subordination of the minister to the congregation. Feelings of personal sinfulness had periodic airing at revivals, but they were held by men from outside the community.

The turn of the century and the war years carried the farmers and farm technique still farther away from their simple beginnings. People found it satisfying to look back on the way things had been done and see how they had changed. Efficiency had been introduced everywhere and had become as much a basic value as work itself. The horse was displaced in the field by the tractor and on the road by the automobile, not because the

[22] *Ibid.*, Feb. 25, 1899.

horse could not do the job, but because it was slow and "old timey." The farmer had dealt so long in terms of work and time that economy in either was desirable, not just as a means to something else, but as an end in itself. If you could cultivate two acres in the time it used to take for one, that was progress, no matter what was done with the time saved. If you could grow two ears of corn where one grew before, that was progress, even if you made no more money thereby. Farming innovations were motivated by the philosophy of production, which had always been operative, lucrative, and satisfying.

In 1909 the county supervisors met with those of three adjacent counties and started organization for the construction of a huge intercounty drainage ditch which would make thousands of acres of land arable. Thus, the lands considered waste by the first settlers were brought under cultivation through the foresight and local initiative of the next generation. Such joint enterprise did not imply any subordination of individual interest to that of the group. The farmers involved were interested for what they themselves could get out of such a project.

The Hardin County Improvement Association was formed in 1916. This forerunner of the farm bureau was motivated by the same conviction that co-operative action gave good returns to the participating individuals. The story of all co-operative efforts in the county has been the same. When advantage to the individual stops, the cause or goal of the group means little. Lip service, expressing ideas which emanated from politicians and educators, is given to the proposition that all farmers' difficulties are due to the fact they do not co-operate. However, few acts portray any conviction that group interests should come first. This does not mean that co-operative efforts are *per se* doomed to failure, for where they are to the economic advantage of the members, such enterprises have done well.

The minutes of the Hardin County Farm Bureau board of directors give a picture of the farm scene during World War I. When first formed in 1916, the bureau's forerunner had members from all the townships but Concord, Sherman, and Buckeye, all in the western tier of townships recently settled by immigrant stocks. Members included many nonfarmers, such as bankers, veterinarians, storekeepers, sheriff, and editor.[23] The superintendent of schools co-operated with this new organization by furnishing an office and secretarial help. The interests of this first organization apparently lay in corn-demonstration plots, alfalfa demonstrations in each township, a county exhibit at the state fair, and a boys' camp for the county fair. In 1917 a farm bureau picnic and home demonstration work were features added to the program. The next year poultry work and a pig club contest were inaugurated.

Two thousand acres of wheat were required of the county during wartime, but only one thousand acres were sown. "Men are afraid winter will kill it out. Others give the reason that they have no ground." The county grain-yield report for 1918 shows only 60,453 bushels of wheat harvested in comparison to 2,045,143 bushels of oats. In 1874 the county had raised almost a half million bushels of wheat. The war need for wheat did not alter the shift to oats.

Calls for men, for work, and for farms to rent were coming into the farm bureau office. Each member of the farm bureau was asked to designate the number of corn pickers needed. The Department of Agriculture questionnaire as to war shortages in the county revealed the need for 183 farm laborers, seventeen part owners, one sole owner or manager. Thirty corn huskers applied for work at the office. "When men are through with corn-picking help they should call their neighbors or send help to the county agent. We do not want the corn pickers to leave until all the corn is in."

Rising produce prices and land values after the war gave sudden impetus to a speculative trend which farmers had felt more or less since the settlement days, when they abandoned homes in the East in an all-out gamble on lands in the West. Suddenly, the drive to get wealthy seemed to become feasible

[23] This represented a good-will gesture rather than any community of interest. This group still joins but never attends meetings. In 1939 the county auditor told a farm bureau meeting that the organization should stand on its own feet and not solicit memberships in town.

in terms of the old economic factors of credit and income. Acquiring extra land to produce an income for retirement appeared easy.

By 1920 land which was ordinarily worth about one hundred dollars an acre was selling for four hundred dollars; the best land was sold for as much as six hundred and even the poorest sold for two hundred dollars an acre. Many older farmers mortgaged their farms and bought property in town, to which they retired. More commonly, farmers mortgaged their land to acquire more land, also heavily mortgaged. Farms were sold and resold, the price rising and another mortgage being added with each transaction. Four or five mortgages on a single farm were not unusual. With the collapse of the produce market, obligations on debts could not be met, and there was a wave of foreclosures. Some tried to keep all they had acquired and lost it all. Others let some land go and saved the remainder. Those who had not speculated had no trouble meeting taxes during the depression, with money saved during the boom times, but such was the uncommon instance.[24]

Two opposing life philosophies, both present in the county, resulted in different reactions to the economic scene. That described above is typical of the Yankee stocks. The German and Norwegian elements in the population were more inclined to value their immediate possessions and ways of life over the speculative advantages of future "advancement." They wanted to acquire farms for their children, but not at the risk of losing their own farms. Further, their desire for land was more limited than was the unbounded drive for profit of the other farmers. There was greater satisfaction in the present for these immigrant stocks, who were considered backward by their neighbors.

The different reaction to the land boom exhibited by the immigrant and the Yankee stocks is reflected in the greater amount of land selling which occurred in the more preponderantly Yankee townships. Taking the number of farm sales by townships, during the height of the boom, one can express this

[24] Mr. J. D. Leonard of the Hardin County Abstract Co. is the source for this information.

number of transactions as a percentage of the number of farms in the township. The percentages of the rural-farm population represented by immigrants and their children are also available for the epoch.[25] Correlating the percentages of farms sold (range: 9.3 per cent to 33.3 per cent) with the percentages of Yankee rural population in the various townships (range: 14.9 per cent to 93.4 per cent), one arrives at a coefficient of correlation of +.57.

Inspection of township data shows one glaring exception to the above generalization. Providence Township, with the greatest preponderance of Yankee stock, shows the fourth lowest percentage of land sold. The population of Providence Township is almost completely Quaker. The religion did not forbid land sale any more than the German Lutheran Church did. The strongly organized religion was, however, another indication of conservatism and a focus of community solidarity. These factors tended to restrict participation of both immigrants and Quakers in the land-selling activity. If Providence Township is removed from the correlation data, the coefficient rises to +.71.

One further fact should be noted in connection with the land-boom sale of farms. The townships in which immigrant stocks make up more than one-half of the population include all of the best land in the county and almost three-quarters of the better land.[26] Land value might conceivably be the determining factor in the number of sales. If, however, one considers only those townships with the poorer land, the preponderantly immigrant townships still participated much less in the land-boom selling than did the Yankee townships on the same sort of land.

When the mortgage and insurance companies, who held the bad farm debts, foreclosed and sold the farms to other farmers,

[25] Population make-up was taken from the 1915 census of Iowa. Land sales were secured from the registered land transfers between January 1 and December 1, 1920. Data on the number of farms were not available by townships for the period in question. The 1939 figures were used. The number of farms in the county has not shown marked change. There were 2,129 farms in 1920 and 2,062 in 1940.

[26] Data on land values were obtained from the county auditor.

individual farmers were hurt, but the general social organization continued as before. But, as has been pointed out, few farmers were in any position to buy land after the collapse. This meant that farms were sold to absentee city owners. If this trend had been allowed to continue, the whole ownership and tenancy pattern of the area would have been radically altered in a direction which has proven undesirable in other areas. Government loans and legislation stopped the evictions and wholesale land transfer.

Another socially significant development occurred at this time. The Collins Mortgage Co. had to foreclose so many farms that they changed their name to the Collins Farm Co. One year they tried to make their investment pay by moving machinery and gangs of men from one untenanted farm to another. The scheme did not work out, largely because the farms were not contiguous, and the farms are now operated by the tenants of the company which took over the Collins' insurance paper. Had the plan succeeded, it would have utterly altered the complexion of farm life.

After the boom was over, the general population make-up and tenancy picture had not changed to any marked extent. The 1930 census of the United States shows the same relative number of immigrants and their children in the different townships, allowing of course for the death of the original immigrants. According to the 1925 census of Iowa there were 209 more owner-operators in the county after the land boom than before, although the actual number of farms had not materially changed. There was a marked shift from cash rent to a cash and share arrangement. After the depth of the depression there was an increase in the number of farms and the number of owner-operated farms went back to its 1915 level. Tenant farms increased markedly. There is a noticeable tendency at present for persons from outside the county, who are nonfarmers, to invest in Hardin land.[27]

[27] Leonard mentions recent purchases of two farms by a man in Colorado and three by a man in Maine. N——— mentioned seven bought by a former Hardin County man now in Idaho in the grocery business. N——— has four of his own.

III
THE SOIL AND THE PEOPLE

HARDIN County is situated almost in the exact center of Iowa and is included in three of the five soil areas of the state.[1] In soil types it includes those prevalent in other parts of the corn belt as well. Various glacial deposits cover the entire county. The Wisconsin drift which covers the western four-fifths of Hardin is so recent, geologically speaking, that it is still topographically immature. The land is almost flat with little natural drainage. The eastern fifth is an older deposit and is well drained. The Iowa River cuts through the northern and eastern part of the county so as almost to divide the areas mentioned above. Various tributary streams extend westward over the prairie.

The predominant types of soils are Carrington loam (35.2 per cent), Clarion loam (19.5 per cent), Tama silt loam (13.2 per cent), and Webster silty clay loam (10 per cent). These soils are very fertile, being well supplied with nitrogen, with organic carbon, and, to a more limited extent, with phosphorus. They are all acid and require liming with the exception of the Clarion loam. Manuring and the addition of acid phosphate give very advantageous results in increased yield. The farmers now recognize these soils as those best adapted for agriculture, while the rough steep slopes of the larger streams are utilized for pasture. The influence of soil type on land use goes no further than this, although some soils are better suited to specific crops. A farm with Webster soil, well suited to corn but poor for small grain, will be put in both types of crops following the general pattern of agriculture of the area.

The climate shows a markedly wide range of temperature, but is very favorable for agriculture. The range of monthly temper-

[1] Source materials on soils are from T. H. Benton and W. W. Strike, *Soil Survey of Hardin County, Iowa* (Washington: U. S. Dept. of Agric., 1923) and W. H. Stevenson and P. E. Brown, *Soil Survey of Iowa, Hardin County* (Ames: Iowa State College, 1925).

ature means is from seventy degrees to eighteen degrees Fahrenheit. The extremes are 103 degrees and −35 degrees Fahrenheit. During periods of extreme cold and little snow wheat sometimes is killed, but such conditions are rare. The mean annual precipitation is 34.55 inches with extremes of 54.66 and 9.52 inches. Droughts are infrequent and of short duration. The growing season is five months long, beginning May 4 and is of ample length to allow the maturation of crops.

The major crop of the county is corn, over one-half of the cropland being put in this grain.[2] The yield usually averages between forty-five and fifty bushels to the acre, the recent introduction and general acceptance of hybrid varieties causing a general increase. The highest yield in the county was 135 bushels to the acre on one farm in 1939. Of the corn 90 per cent is allowed to mature in the field and is then husked for grain. The remainder is cut for silage or fodder or is "hogged down."[3] The greatest part of the grain is not marketed, but is fed to livestock.[4] The next most important crop is oats, which is sown on a third of the cropland and yields upwards from thirty bushels to the acre.[5] About half of the oats crop is marketed, which throws the county into the cash grain type of farming area.[6]

The corn is fed largely to hogs, and the prevalent attitude is that it is thus more profitable to "manufacture the corn into pork." There were 75,111 hogs on Hardin farms in 1935.[7] Although the general trend has been toward more hog raising since the time of settlement, the yearly production has been irregular. Weather and market conditions, particularly the ratio

[2] County AAA office records, 1936–47: total cropland, 270,571.6 acres; corn, 145,181.7 acres—142,574 acres in 1932 before restriction under AAA, Lauren K. Soth, *Agricultural Economic Facts Basebook of Iowa* (Ames: Iowa State College, 1936).

[3] *Ibid.*, p. 64.

[4] C. L. Holmes and C. W. Crickman, *Types of Farming in Iowa, II* (Ames: Iowa State College, 1938), p. 204.

[5] 84,675 acres in 1933, Soth, *op. cit.*

[6] Holmes and Crickman, *op. cit.*, pp. 205 ff.

[7] Soth, *op. cit.*, p. 44. There were 104,083 hogs in 1930.

of the price of corn to that of hogs, are responsible for these variations. Cattle are raised for milk and are also fed for market, there having been 51,195 head on farms in the county in 1935.[8] Of that number 22,121 were cows and heifers over two years old and 16,620 were milk cows. About one-third of the feeder cattle are bought at livestock markets outside of the state for finishing on the farm. The other two-thirds are home-raised. The county is divided in its emphasis on stock raising. Most farms specialize in hogs, but keep a few milk cows and fatten a few head of cattle each year. Farmers who have a large amount of permanent pasture find cattle raising better suited to their farms. As this type of land lies along the river and streams the cattle raisers are more concentrated in the eastern part of the county through which the Iowa River flows. It is for this reason that the county is divided between the central hog and eastern hog and beef-cattle areas of Iowa and the grain and grain-and-grass areas. Sheep raising has increased steadily since 1928, so that there were 26,196 head in 1935.

In addition to these major farm products, soy beans have grown rapidly in popularity because of their high protein content. They are usually cut for hay, but some are threshed for the beans. Other hay crops are clover, alfalfa, and timothy, usually in mixtures, particularly clover and timothy. There is a specialization in popcorn in a limited area around the town of Hubbard, which is not characteristic of the corn belt. Garden vegetables are grown for family consumption on all farms.

Farms are most frequently a quarter section in size and one hundred and sixty acres is generally considered a family-sized farm.[9] More than 80 per cent of the farms fall between an eighth and a half section. Those townships which are cut by the Iowa River and its major tributaries show a lower average farm size.

[8] While the number of hogs had decreased from 1930, the cattle had increased from 36,374 head.

[9] The average farm size was 156.7 acres, according to the *U. S. Census of Agriculture*, 1935. County AAA records for 1939 give an average of 156.5 acres. Almost one-third of the farms in 1935 fell in the 140 to 174-acre range. 100 to 174-acre farms have been the mode in Iowa since 1910 at least.

Thus, Hardin Township has an average of only 128.5 acres to a farm, whereas Grant which is uncut by any large stream, has 178.2.

According to the plat book the small farms are clustered in large number along the waterways. Some of the largest farms are also on the river, illustrating the limitation on absolute geographic determinism. Considered from the point of view of the social factors involved, the poorer soils for grain crops have reduced the land value so that the marginal owner with small capital is forced into this area. Many farmers who came to Hardin from poorer areas of Tennessee, North Carolina, and Missouri have settled on this land. The popular recognition of a different social type along the river is seen in the term "timber rat," which is often applied to them. Yet, intermingled with this group are many exceedingly large land holdings taken up by cattle raisers, who desire the permanent pasturage. No one raises cattle exclusively, but the big cattle raisers feed all the produce which they raise and usually have to buy feed in addition.

Large towns also usually have small farms clustered about them, shading into the house lots and gardens of the town itself. Ackley is the notable exception to this, and the concentration of German families here may be one of the contributing factors.

The farms are operated by both owners and tenants. Although the number of farms in the county (2,260 in 1939) has hardly changed since 1890 (2,101), tenancy has increased steadily, so that 54.5 per cent of the operators were in this category in 1935.[10] This shift is not recent, but was most marked between 1900 and 1910, when tenancy rose from 35.1 per cent to 44.5 per cent. Tenancy in Iowa, however, bears no relation to that of the South. An Iowa farmer must have several thousand dollars worth of animals and equipment before he can even become a tenant. Further, it is quite possible for him eventually to acquire a farm through tenant farming.[11] In 1939 one tenant had a twenty thousand dollar investment in finishing three

[10] Twenty-four and seven-tenths per cent in 1880, U. S. Census.

[11] See Chapter IV.

hundred thousand pounds of beef for market—an extreme case but illustrative.

Share cropping is the most prevalent tenancy arrangement.[12] Under the grain share system, the tenant furnishes machinery and stock and pays the owner half the corn crop, 40 per cent of the small grain, and cash rent for pasture and hay land. A variation on this is stock sharing, in which the owner pays for half of the stock and seed and shares equally with the tenant in all profits. Only about one-eighth of the share tenants are on stock shares although they profess a preference for it. The farm owner is always responsible for the upkeep of farm fences and buildings irrespective of the type of tenancy.

Within the above tenancy system there are two special situations which are important. One is that in which the tenant is the son or some other close relative of the owner. Kin tenancy varied from 18 per cent to 40 per cent of all the tenants in two townships, which probably represent extremes.[13] In the latter township almost a quarter of all the farms are farmed by kin tenants. This is Concord Township, which is largely a Norwegian settlement. The greater family and community solidarity of this culture group and its different attitude toward the land is well expressed in this tenancy pattern. Three-fourths of the kin tenants in Concord are on share arrangements rather than cash rent, whereas the reverse is true of the kin tenants in the other township (Pleasant). Kin tenancy offers greater security of tenure to the farm operator under either cash or share arrangements.

Just the reverse is true of tenants on corporate-owned farms. Corporations own 10.7 per cent of all the farm land in the county. Of corporate ownership by townships, 10 per cent is the mode and the extremes are 21 per cent and 2.5 per cent. The

[12] In 1930 cash rent and various share arrangements were equally popular. If the 1935 AAA participants (76 per cent of the total) are a fair sample, share tenants made up 46.5 per cent of all farmers. In 1930 they constituted only 25.7 per cent. Cash-rent tenancy fell from 25.6 per cent to 8 per cent in five years in response to unsettled market conditions.

[13] 1939 AAA records on all farms in Pleasant and Concord townships.

amount of corporate ownership does not correspond exactly with the amount of participation in the land boom, for the farms taken over by some insurance and loan companies have been sold back to farmers in large part. Nevertheless, those townships in which land selling during the boom was most marked are those which have the greatest number of corporate-owned farms. The fewest are in areas of little boom selling.

The disadvantage to the tenant of corporate ownership is that many of the companies are desirous of getting out as much of their investment as possible, and they try to do this by neglecting improvements and by pushing the sale of the farm. The tenant never knows when the sale of the farm will force him to leave it. The corporations will sell up to March, and it is then too late for the tenant to find another farm as most changes are made in the fall. This results in general neglect of the farm, which draws poorer tenants, and cropping systems ruinous to the farm are employed. Participation in the program of the Agricultural Adjustment Administration has retarded wholesale cropping, but the ill effects on farm and tenant morale are obvious. The passing of a state law requiring that several months' notice be given the tenant before he can be asked to move resulted in such notification being sent to all tenants with the understanding that they could stay on in the event that the farm could not be sold.

For the county tenancy system as a whole, the length of tenure is apparently suitable. The minimum desirable number of years is considered to be two, and the 1935 agricultural census shows that 70.5 per cent of the tenants have been on their present farms for at least that period, while 41.7 per cent had been on five years or more. Uncertainty as to tenure, however, is just as disastrous to the society and to the land as an actual system of short tenure.

The farm household is small. There are an average of 4.5 persons in the rural farm dwelling and about the same number of persons in the family.[14] The fertility ratio for the rural farm

[14] In 1920 rural Iowa averaged 4.3 persons to a dwelling and 4.5 members to a family. Iowa stands below United States averages in this respect and is

population is low but is more than sufficient to replace the population.[15] The towns of the county do not maintain their population through procreation, but this is partly due to selection, for many farmers take up town residence when they retire. The county as a whole slightly more than maintains its population. According to a study in a near-by rural area the modal number of children in completed families is two, and the average is three.[16] The business men in the rural town most frequently had only one child, although the mean was 1.6.

The population of the county has remained fairly constant since 1900, when settlement was completed. Some decline occurred during the last two decades.[17] The rural population, both farm and nonfarm, experienced an absolute decline.[18] Relative to the total population the rural farm population decreased from

unusual in that the rural picture is the same as the urban. C. F. Curtiss, *The Population of Iowa, Its Composition and Changes* (Ames: Iowa State College, 1930), p. 57.

[15] Ratio of the number of children under five years to one thousand women between twenty and forty-four years: rural farm, 594.4; rural nonfarm, 430; urban, 404.1; total, 494.4. Permanent replacement requires a ratio of 444.

[16] Earl H. Bell, "In the Wilderness, A Study of Contemporary Life." Unpublished dissertation, Univ. of Wisconsin, 1931, pp. 139–41. Data consist of ninety-eight completed families, including sterile unions.

[17]

Year	1940	1930	1920	1910	1900	1890	1880	1870	1860
Population	22,530	22,947	23,337	20,921	22,794	19,003	17,807	13,684	5,440
Number of farms	2,062	2,179	2,129	2,235	2,294	2,101	1,930	...	404

[18]

	Rural	Open Country
1910	18,128*	11,435
1930	15,635*	10,327

* This change is not as marked as it seems, for Eldora went into the urban category during this period.

55.1 per cent to 45 per cent between 1910 and 1930. This shift in preponderance was due more to immigration to the county towns than to emigration from the open country. The small towns remained much the same, and Iowa Falls and Eldora absorbed the population.[19] The actual decline of the rural farm population is due to smaller families and fewer hired laborers. Improved economic conditions have allowed the movement from the farms of grown children, who were kept at home during the worst of the depression.[20]

19

	Iowa Falls	Eldora
1910	2,797	1,195
1930	4,112	3,200

See also footnote 17 for county population growth.

20 Decline in rural farm population: 1910–20, 6.3 per cent; 1920–30, 3.8 per cent; 1930–35, 4.2 per cent.

IV

FARM LIFE

Rural life no longer runs its course in separate and largely independent communities. The farm family participates in a number of social spheres. Around the neighborhood are the trade areas of the small town, the large town, and the city. There are no marked boundaries to these regions and even the limits of the neighborhood are somewhat indefinite. The neighboring families which co-operate in threshing are bound by varying friendship ties. With the exception of the threshing "ring," there are few compulsive factors forcing neighbors together. Other sorts of co-operative work are largely unnecessary, and amusement finds outlets less spatially determined. One hears much more of "neighbors" than of "neighborhoods." A farmer may "neighbor" with some family a mile down the road and ignore the farmer next to him, not because he does not approve of the latter, but simply because he follows the dictates of personal preference and congeniality. As contiguous farms are now operated independently of one another, neighbors no longer have as many interests in common. The automobile has also been responsible for releasing the farmer from the necessity of social intercourse with any of his immediate neighbors. Relatives and old friends are now sought out, without regard for distance. Although visits to parents, particularly in town, have probably become more frequent than they used to be, the total amount of visiting of all sorts has declined in favor of motion pictures, shopping, or simply driving. These changes have all had a disruptive effect on local neighborhoods.

Farmers still borrow from one another as neighbors. Owing to the scarcity of teams, horses are frequently borrowed, and there is some exchange of cheaper farm machinery, but in the words of one farmer: "If a man never has to borrow, he does not have to lend either." Even work which is "traded" between neighbors, such as that at threshing time, is carefully calculated, so that anyone receiving more man-hours assistance than he renders must make up the difference in cash. Nevertheless, there is a very definite concept of what constitutes a good neighbor. Certainly, willingness to lend a hand in case of unusual ill fortune is included in the concept. Instances of a group of friends picking corn for a sick man are not infrequent. Even here the line is finely drawn. If the man was considered rich enough to hire labor or if it was felt that he was a ne'er-do-well, aid would not be forthcoming. In the latter instance, the responsibility for assistance, although felt locally, would in actuality be transferred from the local group to the wider community, in this instance the county.

The farm, county, state, and nation present a series of social spheres of increasing amounts of potential power. Rural ideology delimits quite clearly the proper spheres of activity of each social unit. In general, no regulation by the larger unit is considered proper if it can be adequately regulated by a smaller one. When a problem becomes recognized as too great for one unit, it is then felt to require regulation by the larger social group. It will be seen that with respect to social action groups, all those larger than the farm are politically defined. The neighborhood has practically ceased to act as a unit. The decline of the neighborhood as an entity has increased the dependence of the farm on the county.

A few illustrations will clarify and bear out these facts. The early settlers felt that law and order were a social obligation which they preferred to regulate on a county basis. The community did not hesitate, however, to "assist" the formal authority by vigilante activity. In education, the school was at first financed on a subscription basis. Relief was handled by the community church. Both of these functions were very early passed to the county unit. In recent years state welfare was tried and rejected by Hardin people. In spite of the money which state relief obviously poured into the county, local administration of local relief funds was felt to be sufficiently successful.

Farmers sell produce to distant markets. If prices are low,

they expect that something should be done by legislation to raise them. But when the legislation consists of altering local farm practice, the cure, even if effective, is deemed of dubious value. The state provides higher education outside of the community, but county schools are not tampered with. When the government regulates railroad prices it does not say which of the farmers may ship by rail. The county may support a library, but it cannot dictate the books to have in the home. Popular thinking sees an increasing tax burden as the only legitimate control of the individual resulting from services of the various government units.

The next larger area of social significance beyond the neighborhood is the township. These arbitrary regions were formed as political and tax units, and they have continued to serve largely these functions. In recent years they have also become units of organization of the Farm Bureau and the AAA. Both bodies have encountered certain difficulties due to the fact that no actual social unity exists within the township. Some states have organized the Farm Bureau on a natural community basis. The only advantage claimed for the township system by the Hardin County agent is that each unit has approximately the same number of farms. The fact that the Farm Bureau membership varies greatly in the different townships is ignored. Actually, the failure to get members in some townships is due to community divisions within them.

It should be noted that as arbitrary as the township divisions are, they show a general tendency, either singly or in pairs, to become trade areas of small towns. There are fifteen townships in Hardin County, all of equal size with the exception of two of the most northern ones which divide the area of three normal townships between them. With only one exception, there are small towns or railroad stops in each township. In their development some have outstripped others, so that today some of the rail stops have only a grain elevator and a store, and others are towns of several thousand people. There are ten towns having a population of more than two hundred persons. Eight of them range from that to fifteen hundred.

Eldora and Iowa Falls have populations of, roughly, three and four thousand, respectively.

These varied towns are scattered so that no farm is farther than eight miles from one of them. The five townships which have no towns within them are all near towns. In three of these instances the towns are just over the township boundary. The two other townships lie next to Hardin Township, where Iowa Falls is situated. It can readily be seen that the greater "pull" of this large town has discouraged the growth of smaller centers. Recent years have seen the rapid growth of the two large towns, while the smaller ones have barely held their own.[1]

The small town used to be the shopping and shipping center, the focus of the church, and the residence of retired farmers. The automobile has so increased the shopping range of farmers that now the large town has become dominant.[2] Whereas the trade area of the small town is still a social entity, so that farmers identify their location by reference to the name of "their town," its importance is decreasing. The only shopping done in the small town is of such an imperative nature that there is not time to go to the larger centers. The general store and the filling station can just about hold their own under such conditions, but all other trade has moved to the large town or is doing a poorer business than are the large town competitors.[3] Bell noted that it is a common Saturday practice to shop in the large towns and to return to the small one to fraternize with friends in the evening.[4]

[1] From 1910 to 1930 Iowa Falls and Eldora increased 50 per cent in population. Five of the small towns lost 5 to 10 per cent of their population between 1920 and 1930.

[2] Commenting on the rebuilding of a rural neighborhood church, actually undertaken as a result of a church squabble, a farm wife says, "It was a mistake to rebuild a rural church. Those people all trade and send their children to school in Eldora."

[3] *Consumers Market Data Handbook, 1939*. Comparison derived from the numbers of stores and gross sales in Iowa Falls and Eldora and the rest of the county by kinds of business.

[4] Earl H. Bell, "In the Wilderness, A Study of Contemporary Life." Unpublished dissertation, Univ. Wisconsin, 1931.

While the small town is still distinctly rural in character, the town of several thousands is the source of new social types, new ideas and values, and new customs. The townsfolk do not consider farmers to be inferior to them. Public education has done much to eradicate differences in training between town and farm, but the farmer is still a distinct social type. The most striking fact is that urban dominance is manifest in the desirability of city and town traits for the rural population. For the older generation this is expressed largely in the desire for the material culture, the "conveniences," of the town. Youth finds the whole gamut of urban interests and ways of life to its satisfaction. Both seem to feel that higher attainment is possible in the city and that the future of the farm lies in making rural life like that in town, while retaining the freedom of activity of the farm. The open rural-urban conflict is gone, but the self-consciousness of the farmer is evident in his elaborate attempts to describe farming as an industry—to justify his livelihood by identifying it with urban enterprises. In actuality, the farmer continues to behave and think competitively toward the city, but the dominance of its ways is a fundamental value which has long been recognized as of major import in rural America.

Hardin County is divided in its spheres of urban influence. Whereas the county seats of many counties have become the dominant trade centers of those counties, the eccentrically placed seat of Hardin County and the local railroad development have produced two centers in the county. They divide the area almost exactly in half. The circulation of the major newspaper of Eldora defines that town's area of dominance as clearly as possible.[5] The county seat draws its trade from the southeastern half of the county, and Iowa Falls draws largely from the remainder. In all of the townships around Eldora Township, the rural subscribers constitute more than 50 per

[5] This definition of the trade area of Eldora coincides with that secured from merchants of the town in a less exact form. It is also significant that the relief administration similarly divides the county. The county agent, residing in Eldora, could name and give the denomination of all churches in the county with the exception of those in the three northern townships.

cent of the total population. This circulation coverage also extends to two other southern townships (Tipton and Grant). The northern sections of the county are practically untouched; they all subscribe to the Iowa Falls paper. The remaining townships in the west are divided in their allegiance.[6] The buying behavior of people in these various parts corresponds to these subscriptions. The more distant from the center, the greater the likelihood that some other trade center will be utilized. Hardin towns draw some trade from adjacent counties as well, so that the Eldora trade area extends to the east into Grundy County for a short way until the "pull" of the larger town of Grundy Center stops it.

Beyond the county limits are the cities of Marshalltown and Waterloo, which draw an increasing amount of rural trade, particularly for clothes. Marshalltown vies with Des Moines in its influence on the county through newspapers and the radio.

Within the county the culture is not homogeneous. One farmer characterized the rural culture pattern by commenting, "You can't put all your horses in one corral." It is true that in Hardin County there exists a marked variety of ways and values of life. Each is a distinct pattern for a particular group. Some of these seem to be changing toward a sort of norm, others are apparently more stable. Even slight cultural differences create social gulfs between various population groups. The most significant differences are based on nationality background, religion, type of economy, and spatial location. The best example of the subtlety of difference is to be seen in the attitude of non-Quakers toward the community of Friends in Providence Township. The ancestors of this group took pride in their severe dress, which set them apart from other people. The descendants continue to be felt as a very distinct group by the county at large, whereas in dress and general behavior

[6] Subscribers to an Eldora newspaper as per cent of total rural families:

Buckeye	14	Ellis	35	Jackson	68	Clay	79
Sherman	26	Tipton	62	Pleasant	83	Eldora	74
Concord	38	Grant	72	Providence	71	Union	57

they are now indistinguishable. Yet the difference of professed religion remains, and their greater conservatism during the land boom has been noted. Commenting on a suggestion that a certain Quaker be invited to speak at a banquet, a farmer was heard to say, "He stands up and talks like he thought, 'I don't want to talk but God has given me a message and I speak it'." Under other circumstances a newspaperman described the Quaker settlement and concluded: "They are nice people *though*, and good farmers." Such comments both illustrate and continue the feeling of cultural difference. The same attitudes are apt to be extended to anyone living in the township, Quaker or not, as there are no longer externally distinguishing features.

Where social in-group lines are drawn on such slight differences, it is not hard to envisage the attitudes attendant upon more marked cultural differences. The descendants of German immigrants have taken over the Yankee speech, dress, houses, manners of farming, and many of the values. They have, however, been fully indoctrinated in their dogmatic Lutheran and Evangelical tradition.[7] Their family organization and values are foreign to many of their Yankee neighbors. The Germans believe more in the subservience of the child and wife to the father, as the manager of the family farm. The whole family works toward the accumulation of additional farms, which are given to the sons when they reach maturity. These differences are interpreted as "bad" by the Yankees, as cultural differences usually are. The German father is viewed as a "Tartar, working his family to the bone," for does not the Yankee remunerate his children and give them independence of action? Even the Yankee youth, which must pay for its farms each generation, resents the German boy being given a farm. The German family-farm system has resulted in distinct areas of German families, often closely related and co-operating. I have already alluded to the effect of the family-farm values on land selling.

[7] One German lad reported never having been permitted to go to Eldora, ten miles from his farm, until he was sixteen years old.

Differences in eating and drinking habits also set this group apart from, and often in conflict with, the Yankee farmers.

The Norwegian story is practically the same. Norwegians, in their way, remain distinct entities. None of the groups remains isolated. There is general social intercourse between the various cultural elements and some intermarriage. Closer relationships are marked in the recent generation. This is, in part, the basis for popular expressions that the assimilation of these groups is practically complete. Assimilation to American national symbols is the important fact for the Yankees. When discussions of this sort arise, attention is invariably called to German families whose sons fought in World War I.

Another subculture which is also important is the distinctive way of life of the "timber rat." Whereas the Germans and Norwegians have been economically successful in the eyes of their neighbors, the small farmer on a marginal economy on the poor river land has not. Judging their success in terms of their own values, these farmers are probably more happy than their richer neighbors. Since they come from even poorer land and are less imbued with the drive to progress, these people have made an adjustment satisfactory to themselves but not to the eyes of the public at large. The difference in economic attitudes is striking in the comment of one "timber rat" who owned a few hens. Said he, "When eggs get up to sixty cents, they certainly are good." The monetary evaluation was there, but he thought not so much in terms of increased profit as in terms of living and enjoying life. Spare time, which might be used at odd jobs for profit, is spent gossiping, hunting, or fishing. In the context of the whole culture, this group is continually under the fire of the "progressive" farmers, to whom such variations from their own standards are abominable. The "timber rat" wants a living, but his demands are more limited.

The farmer of Hardin County does not live solely within his locally generated sphere of thought and activity. He is influenced continually from the reaches of the city and nation, to which he feels an active cultural link in addition to his economic connection. He usually interprets the acts and problems of people within this wider social horizon in terms of his own acts and values. Thus, while he feels himself as a segment in a vast complex society, the focus is entirely egocentric or ethnocentric. This, of course, is a human-behavior characteristic of almost all groups, but it means that all policies of government, industry, and labor are judged on the basis of local prejudices and local effects.

The farmer's most important avenues of communication with this urban and national life are the newspaper, the radio, the moving picture, and personal contacts largely made possible by the automobile. Everyone is affected directly by at least one of these factors, and the great majority of people are affected by all of them either directly or indirectly. The store, various outside representatives entering the county in official capacities, the preacher, the teacher,[8] publications of all sorts, and personal letters fairly well complete the list.[9]

Practically all farmers take two newspapers, a weekly county paper, and a daily city paper either of Marshalltown or Des Moines. These latter are typical urban papers whose national and international news constitute their main interest to the farmer. "The papers never give the straight of it," expresses the general scepticism with which all papers are read. This attitude is probably related to the general distrust of the city. The county paper confines itself to local news. Although there are seven newspapers printed in the county, the *Eldora Herald-Ledger* dominates the southern part of the county as the Iowa Falls paper does the northern part. The *Herald-Ledger* carries special "personal" and "club news" sections for all of the

[8] Education is included as a minor influence for reasons which will become apparent later in this chapter, primarily the system of "inbreeding" and undertraining of teachers. Those exposed to higher education rarely return to the county. The Iowa State College at Ames exerts a real influence through the county agent and, on a minority, through pamphlets and letters.

[9] The description of "the" culture pattern of the county will be continued here largely in the light of the majority group of Yankee stock, admitting marked variations in emphasis between the culture groups delimited above.

towns within the Eldora trade area, leaving the northern and extreme western communities to their own local papers.

The *Herald-Ledger* is owned and edited by a Democrat who tries to publish a nonpartisan journal. As most of the news items and all editorials are written by a sole full-time reporter who is Republican, the policy is often other than that of the editor. The news stories deal with country meetings and occasions of all sorts, special honors to citizens, athletic contests, court, school, and church events, accidents, and fiscal affairs in the county. The editorials are short and place evaluations on local and national events. Often small bits of national or international news, which are unemphasized in the dailies, are included, such as floods in China or the first glider-delivered mail. National items, such as new equipment orders placed by railroads, are made the basis of comments on business conditions. The general function of the editorials is to emphasize rural values through illustration and comment. In addition to the editorials there are three other columns, one consists of bits taken from the columns of other editors, a second, called the "Events of Yesterday," is drawn from the files in ten-year intervals back sixty years, and the third is a woman's column of reactions and reminiscences based on some simple local event, such as the remodeling of a barn.

The local sections from the towns and rural communities include "personal mention" notes and club and church activities. The personal section mentions weddings, anniversaries, births, deaths, illnesses, visits, and visitors. About a third of the club notes are of large secular associations, a third of intimate clique groups, and a third of church groups. The rural paper functions as a sort of formalized "back-fence chat," an institutionalization necessitated by the expanded community. One even finds notes of thanks to neighbors who helped extinguish a fire or thanks to friends who made calls on a fiftieth wedding anniversary. A great deal more mobility is evidenced in the visiting notices than was noted in the paper of 1879. A test column of such items from Eldora and vicinity in a late September issue of 1939 listed thirty-five people who had left their homes during the week to visit friends and relatives or to make business trips. About the same number of outsiders were visiting among the families of Eldora and its environs. Visits and visitors were most frequently mentioned in connection with the larger Iowa cities, but numerous contacts were outside the state and even the country.[10] The amount of travel indicated above is not characteristic of the whole year, since fall is a favored time for visiting. It is becoming increasingly common for farmers to arrange a vacation away from home when work permits. Fishing and hunting trips into Minnesota are frequent.

The advertising in the newspaper is almost all local in character. Individual business houses are represented rather than nationally known products. Trade names appear in advertisements of the local firms, but those of various brands of cigarettes and whiskies, so common in the large urban newspapers, are lacking. When the Eldora paper ran an advertisement of the United Brewers, worded to justify the beer industry as a large wage and tax-paying enterprise, a committee of citizens called on the paper and demanded that the advertisement be withdrawn—without avail. Some people object to the city paper on the grounds that it carries many liquor advertisements, but if the Hardin farmer wants printed national news, he has no control over what he brings into his culture with it. To judge from the 1879 advertising, this is a situation of long standing, but one which the local community still resents.

More choice can be exerted in the selection of radio programs. A study of radio-listening habits in Iowa[11] presents the following facts, probably also characteristic of Hardin County. Of the rural farm families, 85 per cent own radio sets; only 47 per cent have electricity in their homes.[12] A daily newspaper is taken by 91 per cent of the families. Of the men sampled, 57

[10] The thirty-five visits alluded to above, included trips through the Midwest, the Far West, and the Southwest.

[11] H. B. Summers, *The Iowa Radio Audience, 1939* (2d ed.; Manhattan, Kan.: Kansas State College, 1939).

[12] Of the farm families of Hardin County 49.3 per cent had radios in 1930 (Lauren K. Soth, *Agricultural Economic Facts Basebook of Iowa* [Ames: Iowa State College, 1936]). Of all Hardin families 90 per cent had radios in 1939 (*Consumers Market Data Handbook*, 1939).

per cent expressed a dependence upon the radio for important national news, as compared with 21 per cent who preferred the newspaper.[13] Radio advertising is also apparently more successful, for 48 per cent of the farm women, who do most of the buying, recalled a specific product radio-advertised the previous day, and only 13 per cent could do so from newspaper advertisements. There is a marked age difference in dependence upon the radio. The eighteen to twenty-five-year-old group greatly preferred and listened more attentively to radio broadcasts than did their elders.

Rural men spend about three and one-half hours daily listening to the radio, and women listen five hours. There is slightly more week-end listening, but fewer women listen on Sunday. To judge from personal experience in Hardin County, a good deal of what is called "listening time" is time during which the radio is left running and the regular routine work is done. For favorite programs, however, concentrated attention is given. Many farm wives rush certain tasks and plan their work in the morning so as to be able to be seated by the radio during their favorite serial drama. During the week, farmers do most of their listening after lunch and dinner. Their wives are able to listen throughout the day.

The sex difference in program preferences is partly a function of the division of labor. News broadcasts are the unquestionable favorite program of both men and women. Then, in order of preference, women like serial drama, comedians, question-answer programs, and "old-time" music. Men like comedians, "old-time" music, market reports, question-answer programs in that order. The serial drama is the amusement of women during their daily housework. Farm economy is a man's concern as evidenced by 47 per cent of the men, in contrast to 21 per cent of the women, including market reports and talks on farming among their five favorite programs. Religious music and devotionals are much more popular with women than they are with

[13] Rural scepticism of printed news is obvious when one contrasts these figures with the 39 per cent radio preference and 39 per cent newspaper preference of urban men.

men.[14] Urban listeners are somewhat less interested in such religious programs than are rural listeners. Village listeners like devotionals and religious music even more than the rural people do. This fact reflects the concentration of retired farmers in the villages.

In an analysis of the sex-age breakdown of program preferences of combined rural and urban listeners, the religious programs are five times more popular with men over fifty-five than they are with those between eighteen and twenty-five. This should not be interpreted as a trend toward less religion, for such age grading in religious interest is typical of the most religious cultures. Similar age variation is to be seen in the greater preference of youth for comedians and sports. The greater interest in popular music represents a real trend contrasting with the preference of the older men for "old-time" music. Market reports and farm talks find their greatest audience among men from forty-one to fifty-five, the age when such matters are of prime importance. These same age variations in all interests are also general among women.

Other than the newspaper, only a limited amount of printed matter enters the farm home. Copies of any of twelve popular national magazines were in only one-half of the farms.[15] Women's magazines are three times more popular with the rural families than are general magazines. In addition to these national magazines, a farm magazine of some sort is taken in most homes. *Wallace's Farmer* and *The Farmer's Wife* illustrate the general type. These are rarely read completely, but the make-up is such as to appeal to varied interests. Specialty magazines, such as those for dairymen and breeders, are com-

[14] Percentage of men and women listeners to three types of programs:

	Farm Men	Farm Women	Urban Men	Urban Women
Farm Talks	25.4	14.7	3.4	2.6
Religious Music	14.2	35.4	13.2	22.8
Devotionals	8.7	16.4	7.2	10.2

[15] *Consumers Market Data Handbook*, 1939. The ratio is 189 subscriptions per one hundred families in Eldora in contrast to the farms.

mon. News periodicals are entirely lacking except for the *Pathfinder*. The most recent trend, noted by Bell[16] and substantiated by interview in Hardin County, is the growing popularity of the physical culture and the "true story" type of publication. This latter finds its justification in the moralistic note struck in the often lurid stories. Magazines lacking this element are condemned. Books of any description, except the Bible, are rare in farm homes and even more rarely read. A growing library circulation affects largely the school pupils and town residents. The literary standards of the readers are not high.

Motion pictures are another potent outside influence on rural culture. Whereas radio program preferences indicate that farmers use this medium to keep contact with the national culture and economy of which they are a part, some listening is for amusement and relaxation. Motion pictures are attended solely as an escape and release from local conventions. The sex magazines play a similar role. The major motion pictures produced during the depression gave no indication of the economic and social stress of the period during which they were made. Some critics find this strange and unnatural, but the lack of mundane unpleasantness in the films is the very reason that they were popular. Almost every family allows itself one such period of escape every week.[17] Some families go to the motion pictures on a given day of the week. Others attend more as the spirit moves them. Farm machinery dealers use free motion pictures as advertisement, and in summer many small towns have "free shows" to attract potential customers to town.

It is significant that motion pictures are rarely the basis of conversation, except for a passing comment as to their quality. News from the papers and situations in continued radio dramas are frequently discussed in detail, but not the plot of a mo-

[16] Bell, *op. cit.*

[17] Conversation with managers of the Eldora theater and with the two in Iowa Falls, which are the only full-time theaters in the county, indicates a rural attendance of about this magnitude.

tion picture. The content is not felt to be important, but the hours spent in the theater are.

The culture traits evident in the motion picture scenes and often the apparent moral to be drawn are quite foreign to and, frequently, antagonistic to the local values. Among the youth of the county, whose values are more fluid, the direct influence of the plays is obvious. Dress styles, vocabulary, gestures, basic sex mores, and success values can often be traced to the radio and motion picture. Some local selection is possible among radio programs, but practically none is possible in the motion picture. If the farm youth wants amusement at the local theater, he takes what is offered. Fundamentalist revival preachers realize this influence, decry the motion pictures, and exact pledges of abstinence from the few youths who are "saved" during the revival season. It is interesting that even the saved see nothing wrong in the motion pictures, but take the pledge because the preacher thinks they should. Some "harmless historical film" several months later is usually their undoing until the next revival season.

In this discussion of major avenues of urban influences, the automobile is certainly important. At present, practically every family has a car of some description.[18] The automobile is so necessary for the rural man that the relief agency recognizes car upkeep as a legitimate expense for its clients. It is largely through the automobile that the rural laborer gets to work, the housewife does her shopping, and the motion pictures are accessible to the farm. In addition, travel to large cities is possible. Types of entertainment can be sought out, such as dancing, which are unapproved in the small town but which are emphasized in newspaper, radio, and cinema. The wider range of goods in the city satisfies the increased range of desires produced by the city.

[18] In 1936 automobile registration for the whole county showed an average of 126 cars to one hundred families. The 1930 figure for cars on farms in Hardin was 93.5 per cent (Soth, *op. cit.*). Summers' figure for rural-farm Iowa, secured in conjunction with his radio study, was 94.4 per cent.

The car has also developed about it a whole complex of nontravel traits in the rural area. This is particularly true for the generation of adolescents, for whom an automobile has become a virtual necessity. Out of buggy driving has come car driving, as the major vehicle of contact between the sexes. Visits in the home have practically disappeared, and aimless driving of long distances, parking and petting, and "going somewhere" have become major amusements of the young. For this reason the automobile is the bone of contention between the parent and child, who both want to use the car on week ends. Deceit devices are frequently resorted to by the child in order to obtain the use of the car. School activities, either real or imaginary, are the most common justification for "taking the car."

A farm-budget study in Iowa indicates that 10 per cent of the total family "value of living" consists of automobile expenses.[19] Although the sample is probably slightly above the average Hardin income, it gives a good indication of farm family economy.[20] The average net farm income in 1938 was $2,400, of which $1,605 was devoted to family living. Food constituted a third of the value of living and one-half of this was cash expenditure. Cash expenses made up two-thirds of the whole family value of living. Household operation and clothing each made up 11 per cent of the total and furniture and equipment for the house another 8 per cent. Health, donations, and recreation-education each made up 5 per cent of the value of living. Between the several net-income groups, varying from under $1,000 to over $3,000, there was a variation in average cash living expenditure of only $260. It seems probable that

[19] Dorothy Simmons, *Family Living Expenditures of 160 Farm Families in 1938* (Ames: Iowa State College). "Value of living" includes farm produce consumed, house-rent value, and cash expenditures—all for the family, excluding farm expense. The 10 per cent for automobile expenses actually represents but half, as half was charged to farm expense.

[20] Of the farms in Hardin County 10 per cent had a gross income of less than $1000, while 10.8 per cent of the farms considered in the study had a net income below that figure.

those with the greater income divert a greater amount into expansion of the farm economy.[21]

The average cash expenditure for food was practically constant for all income groups. The only cash living expenditures which had a marked relation to income group were those for clothing, personal care, and health. Expenditures for health were higher for families with the lo wer incomes. The most marked differences were in the "farm contribution" to living. This was progressively higher for each higher income group. This situation is largely a reflection of the fact that meat and dairy products require considerable capital outlay before they can be produced.

No comparative material is available by income groups, but it is significant that 82 per cent of all the families canned vegetables, and fruits were preserved by almost as many. The average amount for the families in the sample was 264 quarts. Keeping meat in cold-storage lockers in town is increasingly popular to the extent that 64 per cent of the farmers did so. The slightly fewer who canned meat averaged sixty-two quarts to the family.

The average family household consisted of 4.5 members. Family size had no relation to income group. There was variation in types of expenditure according to the make-up of the household—the number and age of the children. The farm contribution to the value of living is 70 per cent higher in the large households than it is for young couples living alone. As the foregoing has indicated, corn-belt farming carries with it a high standard of living. Relative to other parts of the country, this area ranks as high as any other in the amount of material conveniences.[22] A definite amount of physical well-being accompanies this advantage, yet it is impossible to say that greater contentment is also commensurate.

[21] Insurance and investment expenditure is highest in the lowest income group (seventeen families) in this study. Of all families 86 per cent had insurance of an average face value of $6,436.

[22] Carl C. Taylor, and others, "Disadvantage Classes in American Agriculture," *U. S. Dept. of Agric., Soc. Res. Rept.*, No. VIII (1928).

The breakdown of county taxes illustrates further the major interests and responsibilities of the farmer. For 1939 the county tax levy, exclusive of incorporate town and school district levies, was 11.72 mills. The major items in this are 4.85 for various road funds and 2.75 which includes several poor-relief categories. The farmer is actively interested in good roads, and some of the bitterest quarrels develop over the roads to be improved or the location of new highways. He does not approve of large expenditures for trans-state highways, and his continual plea is for more attention to county and farm-to-market roads. He feels that the tourist and shipper are not his responsibility. Real agrarian interest can be shown for the .68 mills which help maintain the county fair and eradicate bovine tuberculosis and Bang's disease.

The farmer pays .17 mills for library extension, but .42 for care of the same. The painful conclusion is only slightly softened by the knowledge that the larger towns spend up to 1.98 mills on their libraries. These facts illuminate the comments already made on rural reading habits. This does not mean that the farmer is not interested in education, for his tax burden for this item may exceed that for all other county purposes. The lowest school levy was 2.82, probably where a few children were attending primary school, while one consolidated school district levy was as high as 39.43 mills. Farmers without children usually resent the high taxes in consolidated areas, for they feel education is a family responsibility, not a public one such as poor relief. There is no question, however, that high-school education has become more prevalent as a result of the consolidation system.

Taxes are felt to be a financial responsibility of the first order. Collections on county real and personal taxes amounted to 90 per cent of the total in the first nine months of 1939. The farmer takes considerable pride in the fact that government AAA payments are frequently utilized to pay taxes. Obligations of other sorts may remain unpaid under the press of circumstances. This is particularly true of doctors' bills. Many physicians have resorted to having patients finance their medical expenses with finance companies, before the service is rendered, if possible. In Eldora a bulletin is mimeographed weekly, for the benefit of participating retail stores, which lists all the recent car transfers, sales contracts, mortgages, and court suits for the collection of debts. The stores are thus able to keep abreast of the credit status of their clients. This is another good example of the change in the character of the community from the time when the storekeeper was the best informed individual on the financial situation of the farmers ot the neighborhood. Greater mobility and expanding credit systems have produced a situation from which grew the new institution of the credit bulletin.

Almost half of the ninety cases brought before the fall session of the county court involved foreclosures or suits to recover the amount due on notes, for services, on accounts and contracts, and for alimony. The other types of cases are also significant. Fifteen involved automobiles, being in large part arrests for drunken driving during a campaign to stop this danger to the public. Half of the drunken-driving arrests, which carried four-to-six month jail sentences, were of men from the county and only three were from outside of the state. Thirteen divorce suits were heard on grounds varying from cruel and inhuman treatment to desertion and drunkenness. As noted, the precedent for divorce in the county is extremely old.

A few court cases arise from the imposition of moral standards foreign to the transgressor and therefore supported solely by law. Hunting and liquor violations, disregard for a health department quarantine, and some assault and battery cases would seem to fall within that category. The common incidence of larcency[23] and some cases of forgery are notable. The frequency of acts commonly recognized as antisocial is a measure of lack of social integration in communities. These cases in Hardin County all arose in the towns. It is true, however, that the rural poor migrate to town, thus increasing the dysphoria of these settlements.

[23] Eleven cases at the fall session of court.

In the modern farm community of mobility and family independence, the church continues to play an important integrating role. One of the few remaining types of primary association centers is the church group. There are some fifty active churches in Hardin County. Only six of these are rural churches in the sense of being situated in the country. These six churches are served by part-time pastors. As the automobile makes the church in town easily accessible to most families, it is difficult to support a rural church where other types of community life are passé. Contrary to popular American opinion, the church in farm areas has not declined in all rural environments. It may be put forward as a generalization that religious values prosper where the social order which they support remains satisfying to the participant individuals. One would therefore expect rural Iowa to be such a place. It is true that increased mobility and competition between denominations may disrupt organized religion, but what has been said for religious values still remains true. This would seem to be the situation in Hardin County.

In 1926 there were 10,102 church members in the county and slightly fewer are recorded for the two previous decades.[24] The gain is more apparent than real, for it falls somewhat short of keeping abreast of population increase.[25] A gain in total membership is characteristic of Iowa as a whole.[26] The major denominations in the county are those that a knowledge of the settlement stocks would lead one to expect. There are 2,369 Lutherans and 1,639 members of the Evangelical church. It will be noted that these two make up 40 per cent of the total and that they consist almost entirely of peoples of European background. Foreign-born residents and their children make up 34 per cent of the population of the county, which indicates

[24] United States Department of Commerce, *Religious Bodies*, 1926 (Washington, 1930), Vol. I. Total Hardin church membership: 1906, 9,824; 1916, 9,651.

[25] Hardin population: 1910, 20,921; 1920, 23,337; 1930, 22,947; 1940, 22,530.

[26] Iowa church membership: 1906, 825,000; 1926, 1,080,000.

slightly better religious indoctrination by these groups, particularly when it is realized that there are some immigrants belonging to other denominations. The Methodist Episcopal membership of 1,933 includes many farmers, while the Baptists and Congregationalists have fewer farmers in their congregations. The Friends have a small membership and, according to Iowa totals, are one of the few denominations which decreased in size in the score of years up until 1926, while the Lutherans gained most rapidly. It is probable that the Quaker birth rate is somewhat lower than that of the Lutheran and Evangelical families, but in addition Quaker community solidarity is passing along with that of other communities. Older members of the Friends Meeting comment on the difficulty of developing "community spirit" among the young, who prefer to drive to large towns for recreation.

There can be little question that strong sacred sanctions are useful in supporting the social order. When one examines those churches which have the greatest success in passing their ideologies on to succeeding generations one finds as concomitant social traits, family solidarity under paternal dominance, social isolation,[27] and very dogmatic ideologies. This is no accident; these are part and parcel of the social whole of a strong church. The fact that these values are contrary to the "progressive and democratic" ideas of many a man who bemoans the "passing of the church" shows a fundamental contradiction in his culture.

As a result of the dominance of these church-disruptive values in our culture, the urban church has changed its character entirely. The rare urban preacher may become specific in reference to current events to such an extent as to "approve peaceful legal picketing and champion the cause of the under-

[27] A Lutheran minister commenting on other denominations said: "We can live together but we cannot cooperate religiously." The bulletin of the same church quotes a pastor: ". . . as all church denominations, from the time that they permitted the State to take over the education of their children, have labored, at their own dissolution, so the maintenance of our Christian day-school is . . . the foremost factor fundamental to our future existence." The local minister regrets the passing of teaching in German.

privileged," as the local paper reports the Des Moines, Iowa, Methodist Conference to have done. But unless the social structure is such as to give sacred sanction to his words, the preacher may lose part of his congregation. The subordination of the pastor to the pastorate has been shown to have early roots in this area.[28] Those who have fallen away from church attendance still cherish the Bible and its teachings, but individual interpretation is apt to become egocentric and less useful as a social sanction.

From this consideration of how religious values are passed on, one may turn to the manner in which the land itself passes from one generation to the next. To describe for the rural scene any such "system," even though it be prevalent, must perforce neglect the variants. It has already been mentioned that the land system under families of immigrants and their descendants was characteristically different from that of the Yankees. Likewise many farm hired laborers may never acquire land, but as long as they too are cognizant of a system of acquisition, into which they try to fit themselves, it appears to be a real element of the culture.

The farm owner usually envisages the time when he can retire to the small town and live from the income of the farm. That income will be derived from renting the farm to a tenant or from the sale of the farm. As farms are rarely bought outright, the owner would hold a lucrative mortgage while the farm was being paid for. This same procedure is followed even when the buyer is a son or other relative. No father wants to have his living given to him by his son; few sons expect to be given a farm by their fathers, so the system is perfectly consistent with the values of both parties. Parental wealth is usually divided equally between the children upon the parents' decease. This means that if one son has been renting his father's farm, on the death of the father the farm will probably be left so that the boy may retain possession by paying to each of his siblings an amount equal to his own share. In case there were

[28] See Chapter II.

two children this would mean that the one who continued on the farm would have to mortgage the farm for half its value. Loan companies often take the mortgage so as to give the immediate cash value of the inheritance to the inheritors. Local farmers are quick to point out that this system makes the farm pay for itself each generation. As the nonfarm inheritors frequently spend their patrimony, derived from their farm brother's income, in the city, this means that rural wealth tends to flow out of the area of its production. It often happens that all of the boys leave the farm, in which case it may be sold to a son-in-law or to an utter stranger.

Some urban movement, not only of the aged but of youth as well, is necessary to maintain the system because the rural population slightly more than replaces itself. Most of the surplus can be absorbed by the large towns of the county. Wakeley[29] has shown that half of the rural children over sixteen years of age have left their parental homes. One-fourth more girls than boys have left. This leaves a definite shortage of marriageable girls in the county, a situation which has given rise to a club in Hardin which was practically formed for the purpose of match-making. The majority of the young migrants do not leave their home county and four-fifths remain within the state. Girls leave home slightly younger than do boys,[30] but they usually do not move as far. There is a slight preponderance of migrants who have had no high-school education.[31] College training results in marked migration from home only when the junior year, at least, has been completed.

The rural girl endeavors to find employment in town with an eye toward eventual marriage.[32] In town she will have contacts with urban men, if such is her wish, or she can save toward

[29] Ray E. Wakeley, *Differential Mobility Within the Rural Population in 18 Iowa Townships, 1928 to 1935* (Ames: Iowa State College, 1938).

[30] Modal age at leaving home: Girls, 18 to 20; boys, 21 to 24. See also ages at marriage in the immediately following text.

[31] About one-half of the rural children have never been to high school. Less than 10 per cent go farther than high school and very few finish college.

[32] Town girls move to the city in large numbers, leaving a need for girls in town.

the day when she can help set up a rural home. It is not only felt to be acceptable but proper that a young woman should work and save for her future. After marriage the situation is entirely changed, and for a married woman to be employed is felt to be degrading. It is all right for a woman to assist her husband in his business, but to do the same work for an employer is highly improper. These same values hold both in the country and in town.

The young man in the country also begins to work and save, but his opportunities are more frequently in the rural area, often on his father's farm. He starts simply as a wage worker and must remain in this category until he can earn or inherit enough money to make down payments on essential machinery and buy stock enough to qualify as a tenant. As a wage worker he competes with farm laborers of all sorts. There are very few married men with permanent employment on farms.[33] A great many married laborers live in town and depend on seasonal farm employment and odd jobs in town. Young men from neighboring counties and states are often employed on the farms seasonally or the year round. Hardin County employs year-round help on 29 per cent of its farms,[34] which, with harvest work, gives the rural lad ample opportunity.

When a young man is financially able to start farming on his own as a tenant, he must get married. The division of labor is such that there is practically no alternative except hiring an aged housekeeper, which would be only a temporary arrangement. According to the county marriage records for 1936, the modal age at marriage for farmers is twenty-one years and eighteen years for their wives. One-half of the men were married between the ages of twenty-one and twenty-five; a similar

[33] In 1935 figures show only 177 farms in the county with two or more occupied dwellings. Many of these are homes of retired parents, leaving few for hired men. It is doubtful if a married couple is ever taken into the farm operator's house.

[34] This many wage workers, including paid members of the family were reported for January, 1935 (*U. S. Census of Agriculture*) during the slack season. For Iowa as a whole only 18.3 per cent of the farms reported wage workers.

portion of the women married between the ages of eighteen and twenty-one. To judge by the records for 1935 and 1936, there are more marriages in February, a slack period in farm work, and fewer marriages in the busy months of July and August. Large wedding ceremonies are rare. It is very common for the couple to get married, take a short trip to the city, and announce their union in the paper. Weddings are status gestures, more common in town but not beyond rural aspiration.

The young couple, on the basis of their joint savings, start housekeeping on a tenant place. Their life goals are the acquisition of a farm with modern conveniences, the rearing of two or three children with sufficient education to make their way in the world, the development of a group of good friends and acquaintances, and eventual retirement from active farm life. These general life values may be represented as more specific goals, such as "putting John through college" or "buying the north-east eighty," but they represent rather basic desires. To look back on small beginnings, after having fulfilled these desires, constitutes the ultimate of satisfaction. It may be added that the more one has changed from his beginnings, the greater success he is considered to have achieved.

The existing social order permits the fulfillment of these values and presents the social mechanisms for doing so. Not everyone will succeed completely, and not everyone will have the same opportunity to do so. The grown children of farm owners or of tenants on very large farms can make an early start on their way up the "agricultural ladder" of wage worker, tenant, part owner, owner.[35] Children of poor tenants and wage workers are less likely to complete the scale or eventually to

[35] Wakeley, *op. cit.*, p. 302. From a sample of male heads of households, the relation of age to tenancy is seen in the fact that the modal age of tenants was thirty-five to forty-four years and that for owner-operators was forty-five to fifty-four years. The absolute figures tell the same story:

Age	Owner-operators	Tenants
25–34..........	24	124
55–64..........	192	74

secure full quarter-section farms. This division in possibilities is more marked at present than it was a generation ago. The change has been in the amount of capital required to become an acceptable tenant on a good farm—the only situation which offers any opportunity of eventually acquiring a farm. The usual procedure in scaling the agricultural ladder is to move from one tenant farm to another until a satisfactory one is found. Even farms which are owner-operated may be sold if a good opportunity to acquire a better farm is encountered. As a result of the drive to acquire land, even in small amounts, and the undesirability of renting small tracts, the number of owners who operate farms of less than one hundred acres is double the number of tenants on such farms, while the proportion is almost equal on larger farms.[36]

It must be obvious that for the existent system to work satisfactorily, the farms must be sold to farm operators upon the death or retirement of the previous operators. As long as this condition is present, frustrated desires to acquire such farms can arise only from increases in farm size and population.[37] If, however, farms are bought as investments by urban parties and passed on to the next generation as such, this reduces the number of farms available for owner-operators. There seems to be some tendency in this direction at present, but as some farms are always tenant-operated under the existing system, no pressure on the farm market can yet be felt. The types of tenancy and facilities offered on these "investment" farms usually provide an opportunity for the tenant to make money.[38] This does not negate the fact that should such investments become prevalent they would force basic alterations in the farm culture and permit abuses not now possible.

[36] *Ibid.*, p. 301.

[37] At present the local population requires some urban outlet and farms are increasing only slightly in size. The prospect would seem to be for the birth rate to decrease and for the number of both smaller and larger farms to increase gradually, unless urban financial interests enter the field.

[38] The farms are usually of good soil, with good buildings, and stock shares are frequently the preferred type of tenancy. These farms are not to be confused with those owned by corporations as the result of foreclosures.

Within the broad cultural framework, life on the farm is well defined with respect to the part each member of the family is expected to play. The father is responsible for the management and operation of the farm, the mother is in sole charge of the house. She usually has the planting and hoeing of the vegetable garden and the care of the chickens as additional tasks. Consistency of practice shows that even borderline jobs are clearly defined. The man plows the vegetable garden, for that involves the team, and the woman washes milking equipment, for that involves heating water. The children assist their parents, and it is usual for the boys to help the father and for the girls to assist the mother. The older the children are, the more rigid this division becomes. When there is only one child, he or she is expected to help either parent with smaller tasks while young, but the idea of a boy in his teens doing housework is deemed amusing. Force of necessity, wherever labor is limited, may alter normal arrangements so that the hired man may garden if the wife is not well. Women may occasionally help the men with milking, or may even assist in corn picking if the family is poor, but there is definite loss of status thereby. The following conversation illustrates the attitudes with respect to division of labor. A son of eighteen, having finished the morning milking of the herd of cows, asked his mother to telephone to a neighbor about sending over a farmhand for the day. The mother refused, as she was busy, and the boy countered, "If I empty the ashes and feed the chickens, you should do that," to which the mother responded, "You aren't doing those things for me but for your sister" (she had left on the school bus after helping with breakfast).

The money which the woman makes raising chickens is usually considered to be her own, to be used for the house or even for herself. The farm wife often raises as many as a thousand chickens. One woman raised that many from setting hens over the insistence of her husband that she get a mechanical brooder. There is something more in the task than the simple production of chickens; there are satisfactions in doing familiar tasks which constitute a sort of self-discipline through work, which is characteristic of both sexes.

In general, there is but passing interest in the work of the other sex. Husbands will express pride in their wives' success, but they are apt to be surprised at the number of chickens their wives have raised or that the tomatoes have done so well. Conversely, a wife must know the general stage which the farm work has reached so that she can start the womanly chats with "We still have twenty acres of corn to pick. Are you through yet?" Then the conversation can move into the more familiar channels of discussion of "Ruth's new dining room suite."

The family is still a co-operative economic unit, but its solidarity is waning.[39] Remarking on pictures of the family ancestors, the presence of which is a good indication of family solidarity, one woman said: "They are getting further and further back. First they were in the dining room, then the bedrooms, and pretty soon they will be upstairs in the attic." In conversation, the kin relationship between persons is rarely mentioned. Family reunions are still held, but they are less frequent and are increasingly formal.

Many dominant values operate so as to disrupt family solidarity. Every adult works somewhat on a separate economy, the father has his farm, the mother her chickens[40] and prizes at the fair, the son his wages as a hired laborer. The parents do not want many children and are working toward eventual retirement. The children are oriented toward economic independence and separation from the family. Recreation is entirely outside the family group with utter separation of interests between the generations. Since the parents expect nothing from

[39] The reader is reminded that there is a difference between immigrant and Yankee stocks, but both have the same trend.

[40] The father may even complain about his wife's chickens "because they mess up the barnyard," an overt expression of the competition between the spouses.

their grown children, a father would not consider living in his son's house. There is no particular likelihood that the farm will pass on in the family, and if so, it will be by a sale transaction within the family. When we come to the extended family, there is practically no difference in behavior between that toward an uncle and that toward a "good neighbor." This, of course, does not mean that the family has no significance. The contrast between the hired man and "the family" is too strong to permit such a statement. The "home" is still a sanctum of a sort, which is open only to the family, close friends, farm laborers, and occasional personages such as the minister.

The farm household is intimately affected by the sequence of farm activities during the year. There are periods of stress and hurry which even the wife, who is not in the field, must take account of. In summer the men are up at four o'clock and in the field by five. There are extra hands to feed at threshing time. But in winter the family can rise at six, do the chores twice a day, and still have time to visit and chat and listen to the radio.

The accompanying chart depicts the general series of types of field work done during the growing season and gives an indication of their duration. The chart represents work during a normal season on an average corn-livestock farm. Severe weather, unusual mechanization, or economic specialization would obviously alter it. A frequent variant is tame hay grown in place of alfalfa. Harvests may be shifted a week or two, depending upon when they ripen, but the sequence of activities remains much the same. Mechanization has reduced the man-hour labor requirements of the farm. Not only are fewer hands required but more than a month of total growing season is left free of field work. This time is devoted to such tasks as fixing machinery, fencing, repairing and painting buildings, manuring, liming, and cutting weeds. Part of the time saved through mechanization is thus spent on building up the farm and improving its appearance. Such work improves the status of the farmer, although the tasks are not generally to his liking.

	EARLY	LATE
April	Oat seeding—Spring plowing, fertilizing, fencing	
May	Corn planting—Soy bean planting—First alfalfa cutting	
June	Corn cultivating	Corn cultivating
July	Harvesting oats—Second alfalfa cutting—Threshing of oats	
August	Repairing and painting buildings, improving land	Second alfalfa cutting
Sept.	Preparing silage	Farm repair and improvement
Oct.	Harvesting soy beans	Corn picking
Nov.	Corn picking	Plowing, if possible
	EARLY	LATE

The farmers still consider that they have to work all of the time. They are apt to justify the purchase of farm machinery as a means of doing more work.[41] In reality, there is a growing tendency for farmers to take a vacation in early August. The increasing amount of time spent in town or by the radio becomes understandable. Mechanization serves to improve the standard of living, but not solely through greater agricultural production. Farmers abhor bookkeeping, and the actual economic gain resulting from mechanization is unmeasured as long as the machines get paid for.

The monologue of a farmer contemplating the purchase of a new model tractor may sound like a man trying to justify a decision already made. One man began by saying that farmers had so much money tied up in machinery that they never can buy anything else. He then continued by saying that this new

[41] To quote one farmer: "Since the introduction of farm machinery men work harder today than they used to. Seems they're always pressed for time. Some tractors have headlights so they can work . . . well into and even through the night."

model "only costs $950 with all the equipment, and other tractors alone cost $1100 or more." The light character of this tractor should save fuel, there are only two oil changes a year, and there is "nothing to wear out." By this time he seemed to say that contracting for a $950 tractor is the only way to save money. The same arguments advanced by a salesman would be laughed down, for the farmer has the reputation of being an extremely difficult man to "sell."

What then are the real bases of the decision which he is trying to rationalize? They are as much social as economic. The best farmers have tractors,[42] and there is no question that a farmer so equipped works better and faster, both fundamental bases of judgment of any kind of farm work. There is an opportunity to do more farm work, also a locally laudable desire. The type of work will be more agreeable. On the economic side, hired labor will not be required to the same extent, or possibly the farmer can expand his farm base without additional labor. Here is the real crux of the situation. If the farmer could see on his books that the tractor alone more than paid for itself, he would need no other justification for buying it. Actually, he knows he wants one but has some doubts as to the economic sagacity of the move; hence, the rationalizations on the economic level.

In the consideration of other types of machinery, such as threshing machines, combines, and corn pickers, another factor enters in, and that is "custom work." The first man in any locality to buy such machinery pays for the machine in one or two seasons by contracting to work for his neighbors at a price lower than the job can be done by hired hands. This is a tempting situation for the prospective buyer and one of which the salesman makes the most. As more machines are sold the law of decreasing demand soon leaves many farmers overborrowed and overequipped.

Aside from a man's material gain, his land, machinery and

[42] Of the farms 50.7 per cent had tractors in Summers' (*op. cit.*) sample for his radio study. Such farms use horses for corn planting and most wagon hauling.

painted farm buildings,[43] there are other bases of status judgment which are even more fundamental. These lie in the character of the man himself.[44] He must first possess the "basic Christian character" of honesty and sobriety. Further, he must be a good worker. "Time is valuable—well spent it will make you money. If you want to farm, you will have to work," is the admonition given a hired boy. The way one works is also important. "You can tell a lot about a man by watching him work." If he is awkward and apparently lacks interest in his work, "he doesn't have much ambition." The good farmer plans his work in advance, "If you ask him what he is going to do tomorrow, he will know." He must also be frugal in a culture where "economy" means doing without certain things. The man who never spends at all, however, is looked down upon almost as much as is a wastrel. Two of the most common bases of judgment are the cleanliness of the yard and barn lot and whether the man is "up on his work." In winter a farmer usually beds down his hogs on Saturday "so it will look well on Sunday." A tenant on a place that is not "kept up" is likely to be typed by the farm he is renting, even though repairs are not his responsibility. Tenants on such farms are apt to be in a neighborhood for only a short while, so are even less likely to be included in the local social group.[45]

For the farmer there are distinctive satisfactions and dissatisfactions. Harvest may fill a man's heart with joy or he may be "scared to death," as one man expressed his feelings during a corn harvest when the crop was so poor that it was all the pickers could do to fill one wagon a day.[46] Likewise, some tasks

[43] To have a number of fine buildings around a big barn, all painted the same color, and the name of the farm, such as "Fairview," painted in large letters on the end of the barn, is a fine status gesture.

[44] Although the discussion concerns farmers, the same traits, exemplified in different ways, are also pertinent for their wives.

[45] Bell (*op. cit.*) found the average length of tenure on "good" farms to be fifteen years and on "poor" farms only three years.

[46] The equitable climate has made the local farmer expect a good crop. A Nebraska boy working in Hardin gives a cultural contrast when he remarks: "These people take things too seriously. If they had a crop failure, they would go out and hang themselves."

are enjoyable, such as plowing, and others are unpleasant, such as repairing fences. Clampitt, in his autobiography,[47] expressed well the attitude of youth toward farm work in general:

> The joy of life is felt on certain bright April mornings or on glorious October days, but the drudgery is often there; and the boy, who naturally has but little interest in the final outcome of all his labor, must sometimes be oppressed by it.

Those of long farm experience, who turn to urban life, find that the freedom of activity, the variety of work and the lack of nervous strain of farm life have a value which cannot be measured in terms of money. "Work in the city is not hard but it is hard on you," said one farmer who had been a train motorman for several years. Clampitt, in more literary style, wrote with an insight of a lifetime on the farm:

> When driving the seeder or disc, or turning the first furrows, with the smell of the fresh earth in the nostrils and the freedom of the great outdoors all about him, there comes a feeling of exhilaration and a sense of well being to the farmer that the indoor worker can not know. The long term program of the farm is largely fixed and unchangeable but there is more variety from season to season and day to day or hourly. There is a broad languid sense of fulfillment at harvest time which . . . brings a feeling of compensation that is unrelated to either economic success or failure.

In addition to the farm life of the rural population there are numerous special associations and gatherings which provide a different sort of activity. Most of this is in town and constitutes another medium for the diffusion of urban ways. Some of these personal contacts are through long organized channels such as the various lodges which flourished around the end of the last century. The Independent Order of Odd Fellows in Eldora, for example, has a membership of about two hundred, one-half of which is rural. This group is partly the result of the collapse of two other chapters in the county and the transfer of their members to Eldora. As this fact illustrates, the lodge is a fading institution in rural life. Associational life in

[47] Clampitt, *op. cit.*

the large towns is probably increasing, but is becoming more distinctly urban in character.[48] Farm women still take an active part in the various church groups, and the Farm Bureau organization attracts a large group of farm people of both sexes and all ages.[49]

Informal groups are still more common in the rural area than are clubs. Gatherings for oyster suppers, picnics, and the like are frequent. Birthdays, anniversaries, marriages,[50] reunions and housewarmings are made the basis of group gatherings. The various "night schools," conducted by the county vocational schools, attract many farm families both for the instruction and the social gathering afterward. It is not unusual for the country youth to be away from home most of the nights in a week,[51] and parents will usually be out at least once. The weakening of rural primary groups, such as the family and the neighborhood "crowd," and the commensurate growth of amusement spectacles, such as shows and sports, have not given rise to the same proliferation of formal associations that are present in the town and city. Whereas the function of the urban club is apparently to bring together interest groups, the broader base of common interest of the rural people allows such groups to occur and dissolve in a more informal fashion.

Saturday night in town is a perfect example of unformalized primary group activity. In the afternoon or, most commonly, after supper the rural families come to town in their cars. Upon arrival the families separate, the small children accompanying their parents and the mother carrying the baby. The

[48] "Pine Lake Country Club" has 180 members but they are not farmers. The women's card and "educational" clubs (Utopia, Twentieth Century and Sans Souci Clubs, World Wide Guild, etc.) in town attract few farm wives.

[49] See Chapter V.

[50] The "shivaree" is still present but has lost its importance. After the din of automobile horns and tin pans subsides, "you are lucky to get a candy bar nowadays." The newlyweds do not recognize their obligation to treat those who fête the union.

[51] The following is the evening activity of one twenty-year-old young man during one week, church, night school, basketball game, church, basketball, choir practice, Saturday night "in town."

women go to their favorite stores to shop and chat. Aside from the trading which is done, everyone has a chance to talk to friends. As the sidewalks around the court house square are packed with milling people from seven to eleven o'clock, the stores remain open for the trade.[52] The farm people are dressed in regular farm clothes, but these are always fresh and clean. The farmer who comes to town on Saturday night directly from the field feels obliged to apologize for his appearance. As the people move about, groups of acquaintances form on the sidewalks. Girls parade by, arm in arm, and are shouted at by the loitering groups of boys. This results in isolating acceptable double or triple couples of "dates" who later go off in cars. Conversation groups are continually forming, dissolving, and reforming. Friends from over a very wide radius are thus thrown together, and the expanded community does not have to be utterly dependent upon the "personal" columns of the newspaper for grist for its gossip.

Every Saturday afternoon in Eldora, and on Wednesday at Iowa Falls, there is a public auction of all sorts of animals which the farmers have brought in. These auctions constitute a sort of local "stock market" with a good deal of buying with an eye toward immediate turnover at one of the next sales, possibly in another town. Some farmers prefer to sell their finished stock in these local markets because they feel their animals look nicer there than in a major cattle market after a long rail or truck haul. Buyers from the near-by packing houses attend all the local auctions. Farmers also can buy or dispose of half-finished stock through these sales. Many farmers attend the sales to see how prices are going and to talk farming with others. One hundred to two hundred are always on the tiers of benches surrounding the auction pen. Cold drinks can be bought, and farmers often drift in and out of the building and have a generally sociable time. In the late fall and winter there are public auctions of farm equipment, stock, and household

[52] One ten cent store reported that it does a third of its total business on Saturdays. The merchants dislike the late hours to which the farmers force them.

furnishings on farms from which the operator is retiring, moving a long distance or to a smaller place, or being sold out by the sheriff. These sales are looked forward to as entertainment by farmers and, of course, afford the young man an excellent opportunity to secure equipment.

There are other public gatherings based on rural interests. Even commercial demonstrations of tractor plowing draw over a hundred farmers. Annual corn-husking contests still attract considerable interest and about the same group of contestants. Only one-fourth of the 1939 participants had never been in the contest before. It seems, however, that there is more status attached to winning the newer "ten acre corn yield contest" than to winning this older competition. During the summer and fall a series of spectacles, such as the Fireman's Carnival, the Farm Bureau Sports Festival, the Four County Fair, the Waterloo Dairy Congress, and the county and state fairs attract many rural people.

Through stock-judging contests at the county fair, stock breeders can establish and advertise their names and breeds. The local fairs are particularly good for the small breeder who cannot compete with those attracted from distant states to the larger fairs.[53] Rural values find emphasis in the amateur competition for prizes. The fairs are the culmination of the hopes of scores of 4-H Club boys and girls. Adults, likewise, take pride in their exhibits and successes. Even for the nonparticipant observer, the effect is to produce appreciation of good work on the farm and in the farm home. Some community solidarity is developed through the fact that the fair is local, through ball games between town teams, and through school-band exhibitions. Nonetheless, the county fair is having a hard time maintaining itself. Rural youth is more interested in automobile racing than in horse racing, in judging bathing beauties rather than cattle, and in how the St. Louis Cardinals, not the home teams, play ball.

[53] One breeder of Berkshire hogs showed at the state fair, but reported it was hardly worthwhile as he had to show against sows which had never been bred. "A farmer can't afford to do that," he added.

When one examines the established institution for preparing rural youth for life—the school—its emphases are clearly less rural than are those of the fair. This situation has grown out of the fact that the schools, having the task of fitting the growing generation for life either in the country or in the town, have really emphasized urban life. Only recently has any serious attempt been made to adapt the curriculum to the needs of the student who will remain on the farm. Vocational training has too often been a farce in which the farmer's son knew more about farming than his teacher or in which the boy was taught how to make necktie racks or candlesticks. The pupils in the only high school in Hardin County which was investigated were largely from rural homes. Students were allowed to choose, in their last two years, between a vocational agriculture course, in which the manual training consisted of making farm equipment, and a commercial course. "Normal" course training for elementary school teachers, which is popular in other high schools, was not included through lack of demand. Of the boys, 75 per cent elected the agricultural work but only half of all the boys remained in the locality. One is forced to wonder if the other quarter followed agricultural pursuits. Wakeley's study[54] shows only negative correlation between the amount of schooling obtained and the number of young men and women who have left home. The greatest likelihood is that a rural youth who goes to high school is just as apt to spend his life in the country as he is in the city. The vocational course mentioned above is at least an attempt to recognize this fact in the high-school curriculum. There is, of course, no such attempt in the grade schools, which are the complete education of almost half of the children.

The personnel of the schools is also worthy of comment. Most rural grade-school teachers have only a high-school education. All of these teachers in Hardin are local girls, the majority coming from the township in which they teach.[55] The

[54] Wakeley, *op. cit.*, p. 290.

[55] In contrast with this only two of fifteen grade-school teachers in Eldora are from Hardin County. In the high school, which has rural and urban students, half of the teachers are local.

tenure of the teachers is short and the pay poor.[56] Even superintendants are changed frequently. The school organization does not seem to correspond with the high regard farmers have for education except in the relative amount of tax funds devoted to it. From the point of view of orientation, the grade schools put the county boy who goes to the city at a disadvantage, and the high school is apt to spoil the rural boy for a farm.

Part of the reason for this is that high schools are invariably situated in town. The rural child in high school finds all his interests in town. School activities themselves are the predominant excuse for going to town in the evening. Basketball games take on great importance. Schools without gymnasiums are "not worth much." Other sports conflict, in their season, with farm work, but around basketball is formed a community of interest which extends even to adults. School dances have been widely introduced over rural protest. Through all of these avenues rural youth is absorbing urban values and ways of life. One cannot concur, however, with the parental attitude that "the only safe place to bring up a boy nowadays is fourteen miles from town without a car," for the urban trends are part of the cultural fabric of the Iowa farm parents themselves.

[56] In 1939 the average pay for the rural teachers was $64 a month for nine months.

V

SOCIAL ACTION AND CULTURAL REACTION

THERE is operative in all cultures a process analogous to the biological "survival of the fittest." In the cultural sphere it might be termed the "survival of the satisfactory." By this is meant that new social forms and institutions will persist only if they solve more vital cultural problems than they create. Societies are continually in a state of flux, giving up undesirable cultural elements and trying new ways of life. Cultures continually strive toward some sort of equilibrium, often a static one. In the case of the corn belt, there is a striving for a dynamic equilibrium. The dynamic aspect is a concomitant of the basic cultural drive for "progress," which means that the culture must be continually changed in a given direction.[1]

Cultural innovations may solve one particular problem only to create other problems more grave than the original one. The introduction of corn-picking machinery causes increased local relief loads and creates drastic personal problems. However, it achieves culturally determined values through acceptable cultural channels. The simplest farmer feels that something is wrong with the situation, but he lacks the impersonal perspective necessary to bring his values into question. The social planner must not be thus limited; he must not "crusade." He must be continually cognizant of cultural reactions which may have little bearing on his immediate problem but which may be even more important to the functioning of the cultural whole. On that, in the last analysis, will depend the success or failure of the original plans. The following discussion is an attempt to illustrate the numerous ways in which corn-belt culture has reacted to new institutions and set limitations upon them.

[1] From the point of view of comparative sociology, there is a strong possibility that this desire for change is but an indication that American culture is in its adolescence, never having evolved a thoroughgoing adjustment to its environment.

The county farm bureau is an extremely interesting example of how an association, by remaining plastic, has adapted itself to the cultural situation. Its relation to the local culture permits it certain types of action and restricts it in others. From a purely local association interested in promoting a county fair,[2] it has been led by state and national impetus to hire a county agent whose main function is that of a technical adviser for the farmer. The local expenditure for this man was and still is justified basically as a way to make money through improved methods.[3] Because of the position of education in the rural values, the board has usually hired an agent schooled at, and recommended by, the Iowa State College at Ames. This means that the farmers of the county have personal contact with a man who is abreast of innovations in scientific farming. The agent is the most important cultural link between the farm and the laboratory. From the point of view of the relation of the local to the national culture, it must be remembered that the type of innovation which the agent will be likely to introduce will be that approved by the college and its extension administrators.[4] The county agent is further restricted by the fact that he is directly responsible for his job, from year to year, to a local board of farmers. He will do nothing to antagonize them. This is, in actuality, a desirable situation, because the county agent is fully conversant with the local farm culture and will not try to make unsuitable alterations in it, nor will he try to bring about changes too rapidly. In his position the ramifications of a new trait are more apt to be apparent.

There is the additional factor to consider that the county agent is responsible to only that segment of the total county farm population which is included in the farm bureau membership. He therefore tends to represent this group in his opinions

[2] See pp. 24–25.

[3] An ardent bureau member discusses the value of membership: "I saved $9.60 on hog vaccine alone to say nothing of the saving on co-operative insurance and gasoline distribution."

[4] This fact alone is responsible for considerable variation in the reactions of various corn-belt areas to New Deal plans.

and action. The Hardin County Farm Bureau includes about one-fourth of the farmers.[5] Its make-up with respect to tenure is a good cross section of the county.[6] As the membership fee is ten dollars there is probably some overweighting of the bureau with wealthier farmers, but no estimate can be made of its extent. Another variable in the farm bureau pattern is the intelligence and personality of the agent himself. Although even here there is apt to be some reflection of the local farmers, this factor, more than any other, involves pure chance.

In addition to its original function of technical training, the farm bureau has also become a mode of expression of joint farm opinion. Through it the farmers have become a power group felt both locally and nationally. The Eldora paper asks editorially that the bureau not "forget the friends who have aided them in their achievements." In the resolutions of the farm bureau county planning board there is a consciousness of strength: "Farmers can scarcely realize the increased recognition being shown agriculture because of these affiliations or of the power thus being put in their hands."[7] Whereas the early organization had a marked desire to stay out of politics, the present consciousness of strength has led to definite statements on political policy.[8]

The yearly resolutions of the board of directors give much insight into the attitude of farmers toward legislation in their behalf. By 1927 the resolutions are full of pleas for legislation "to put agriculture on a par with industry," or to control surpluses so that "farmers may secure a fair return for their labor." "Equality for agriculture" phraseology was no product of local thought, but it did play directly into the rural feeling of

[5] 1939 membership, 500; 1935 number of farms, 2,239. Boom-time membership was twelve hundred. During the worst of the depression it was two hundred.

[6] From a sample of half of the townships, including those representing known cultural variants, the membership showed 118 tenants and ninety-three owner operators.

[7] 1927 minute book.

[8] Thus, in 1928, it pledged its support "to the surplus control bill vetoed by President Coolidge."

competition with the city. By this time the bureau recognized a distinct change in purpose from "how to increase production" to "how to market at a profit." This did not mean that the farmer was no longer interested in more production but rather that he was most immediately concerned over the falling prices which made production unprofitable. There was no practical suggestion as to what type of legislation would be satisfactory, but a resolution concerning the Farm Business Association is very pertinent to the AAA program: "We believe the Farm Business Association, which keeps farm records and determines what enterprises are more profitable, is better than the 'chain farm proposition' which is a corporation with farms run on the hired-man basis."[9] The "chain farm proposition" is not to be confused with the corporate operation of farms by mortgage companies. The "chain farms" were voluntary organizations of farmers. However, the loss of individual choice of action, under the system, was obviously distasteful.

One concrete method of price control which has always been supported, and frequently has been organized by the farm bureau, has been co-operative buying and marketing. A large part of the produce of the county is co-operatively marketed. The idea of the co-operative is old. All of the early telephone lines and exchanges were established on this basis. The life of any co-operative depends entirely upon the continued price advantage it affords its members. This is apparent in the live-stock shipping associations. In 1923, there were thirteen such associations in the county. By 1928 the farm bureau commented that "the packers' local concentration shipping points will rob the farmers of Hardin County of many thousand dollars each year." The development of local packing houses in Waterloo and Marshalltown, the expansion of buying by truckers, and, finally, the placing of stock on farms through contract with packers sounded the knell of the shipping association. The immediate price advantage which these new methods offered individuals destroyed their associations and created one of the

[9] 1929.

greatest economic problems which the farmers have—that of utter loss of price control on stock. Grain could be held, even by individuals, when prices were too low, but stock must be marketed when finished.

Other co-operatives fared better. In 1939, the thirty-year-old Cow-test Association employed two full-time testers and was expanding. The Wool Pool had secured a price six cents over the local market for a nine-year period.[10] About two-thirds of the grain was sold through a dozen co-operative elevators.[11] Co-operative creameries had flourished, so that about one-half of the cream went to eight such organizations.[12] From 1930 to 1940 the farm bureau co-operative for retailing petroleum products had been gaining ground, aided by state tax exemptions. The prevalence, scope, and long continuity of the co-operative enterprises stamp them as a successful rural institution in spite of their susceptibility to competitive attack from private industy.

Another aspect of the farm bureau work has been in connection with the 4-H Clubs for boys and girls. These appeal largely to adolescents not yet out of school.[13] As restricted as the membership is, the functions of the clubs are important. The emphasis of the boys' group is in stock raising and other aspects of farming. The honor of winning prizes and the cash benefit derived from the sale of good stock attract the youth in directions entirely consistent with the local culture. These club activities compete for the boy's time with other influences, such as the motion pictures, which tend to draw him out of his local culture. The girls' club tries, by means of contests, to further the orientation toward the farm home. Cooking, serving, personal grooming are taught and encouraged. The keeping of memory books as a secondary activity is of dubious value.

[10] The county agent is the source of this and the following information on co-operatives for the period up to 1940.

[11] There were seventeen such elevators in 1923.

[12] There were four co-operative creameries in 1923.

[13] In 1938 there were 134 girls enrolled, only twelve of whom were out of school. The modal age was twelve years (thirty-five girls) and there was none over nineteen years.

The girls are allowed to choose their projects from a given number of possibilities so that their needs and individual differences receive some consideration.[14] A few girls even show stock which they have raised, but the division of labor on the farms makes this unpopular.

The women of the county have their farm bureau work headed by a home demonstration agent whose relation to them and to home economics research is comparable to the position of the county agent. The "home demi," as she is known, reaches all farm women who are interested, just as the county agent does not restrict his aid to farm bureau members. As a result, women in more than one-half of the farm homes are affected in some way.[15] A popular major project was designed to aid home management by giving advice as to the relative nutritive value of different brands of food and planning meals so as to get proper nourishment economically. Instruction in interior decoration and in music appreciation was offered. "Folk games" as a subproject suggests that a nostalgia for the "old days" and for "community solidarity" caused this item to be introduced in an attempt to bring them back.[16] Probably one of the most important functions of this women's work is the creation of local interest groups which meet informally at one another's homes. The township organizations depend entirely on unpaid farm women who act as leaders. Through their activity many groups are being formed in the townships on the basis of the interests of the farm women.

The formation of a rural youth group in the county afforded an excellent opportunity to observe the multiple ways in which

[14] Often the study and work programs are ill-fitted to, or are useless in, a county. Extension programs sometimes seem to be devised as a sort of missionary work unrelated to the needs of the proselyted. Weaving raffia baskets or replacing ancestral pictures with poor copies of "masters" may be time wasted. These statements are not based on Hardin County or even Iowa, but illustrate the latitude left to the extension-program planner.

[15] In 1938, 1311 homes out of 2100.

[16] I do not imply that folk games in themselves are bad. They should be encouraged, where they are present or consistent with the culture, but it is naïve to expect them to play any role in such a place as Hardin.

existent social patterns affect and shape a new social element. This organization was intended for young rural men and women who were out of school but as yet were unmarried. It was designed to provide group activity for those who were too old for 4-H Club work. Several young people who had outgrown the 4-H Club work were responsible for the organization, which was formed with farm bureau aid. Important in the minds of the sponsors, and probably inherent in the desire of the founders, was the desire to provide a social medium through which boys and girls could mingle, form attachments, and eventually marry. As moral values precluded the possibility of forming a group on such interests alone, other activities were tried. Social dancing, which would be ideally suited, conflicted with moral values and was abandoned in a storm of protest. A baseball team was successful but nonfunctional toward the desired end. Drama, singing, debates, talks, and refreshments were old stand-bys with no real appeal to the desired group. A wiener roast was successful, but many left before the ensuing formal meeting. That those who departed left in pairs showed some desired results.

Not only was the youth group faced with problems of finding a suitable focal interest, but there were other problems inherent in the general social patterns. As the group meetings drew from the whole southern half of the county, they were reached by automobile. There was a marked shortage of girls at the meetings, for the boys refused to take their sisters. Girls could not go out unaccompanied, and boys who had girls were uninterested in the organization. In addition, there was an actual shortage of girls in the country due to their movement to town. No constant membership could be maintained as courting behavior caused those couples who had paired off to drop out of the organization. When married they were claimed for the farm bureau membership even if they preferred their own age group. Two other factors were at work. The youth group was on a county basis, which ignored natural communities of interest. Thus the Norwegians were most interested in fraternizing with the youth of their own stock in neighboring counties. A group in Iowa Falls was organized across county lines to advantage. The youth group tended to draw off the leaders of smaller social elements in the county instead of allowing them to activate youth contacts in their own localities. All in all the youth group represented an attempt to fill a cultural need, but its manner of achieving its ends had yet to be evolved.

An analysis of rural relief in Hardin County is illuminating with respect to those factors which made it necessary and illustrates the social concomitants of the relief system. The county director and her staff were all "local girls." For a period up to 1936 there was state aid, so that the county had to employ trained social service personnel. In 1939 the agency used only county funds plus the aid of the various federal agencies: Works Progress Administration (WPA), Civilian Conservation Corps (CCC), National Youth Administration (NYA), and Surplus Commodities. There was a WPA sewing project for women who made clothes for relief clients from material furnished by the county. All families with members on WPA rolls received surplus commodities and medical and dental aid. One-third received fuel in addition to grocery orders. Most of the cases were in the towns and small crossroad centers. Nevertheless, they often represented a rural problem, for the men involved were farm hands. Those on relief neither owned nor rented land, but were married men seasonally employed on the farm or in Iowa Falls industry (two meat-packing companies, one cannery, and the railroad yards). Some of the relief clients lived in shacks on farmers' lands.

Until 1927 there was only a county supervisor of the poor. In that year a special worker came to administer welfare. While the county was receiving state aid, a certain number of cases was necessary to maintain that assistance. The administration in 1939 charged that the case load was previously built up beyond actual need in order to continue this subsidy. To judge from the case records, the refusal of relief was more common in the first years after 1927 when there were more other opportunities. The office was trying to keep down its case load in 1939. When clients were found to have jobs or to be financially splurging, they were cut off, but they soon returned to the rolls.

Socially undesirable elements had to be maintained on the rolls. Their allotments ran slightly lower than the deserving, but they were still a county responsibility. A habitual drunkard, who had been sentenced to jail, made up the WPA time he had lost while incarcerated. WPA was nominally supposed to be for the "worthy," but in practice it was open to all who qualified in residence and poverty. WPA could have been used to fortify social values among those most likely to doubt them—the economically unsatisfied—instead of weakening them by giving the same economic satisfaction to both deserving and undeserving clients. The habitual county relief case going on WPA made that organization more a relief agency than it needed to be. A distinction, emphasized in practice, between WPA and relief could have emphasized proper values. This could have been further carried out if farmers and other employers had applied directly to WPA or welfare agencies for hired help. Thus, the oft-noted refusals of clients to take private employment might have been obviated. This would have given the general community a truer picture of the stated function of WPA.

There were numerous instances of welfare clients refusing two-dollar-a-day jobs. The client on WPA had established work routines, work-group morale, and daily habits, which he did not wish to break for a short-term job. His livelihood was taken care of; there was small incentive to make the little additional money. When WPA employees did hire out on farms, they were often a failure from the farmer's point of view, for they wanted short hours and work which was not too hard. This, in a region which has always esteemed hard work, shows the extent to which WPA set up new and locally undesirable work habits. The welfare department felt that clients of rural background considered WPA less of an economic opportunity. These people were more resistant to employment by WPA and were anxious to work on farms. The type of work and town living were unfamiliar to such laborers. Among farm people on work relief, all had left at least once for farm employment. This seasonal work had been shrinking year after year. Even laborers who had once remained on farms through the winter were being released to swell the winter relief rolls. The tighter economy practiced on the farms made the farmer use help only in season. Farm laborers on relief rarely refused farm work to the knowledge of the welfare department.

Facts which the populace "knew" and which were unknown to the department were such incidents as "WPA sewing circle" shirts bring torn up by the relief client as not being "fit to wear"; "relief" flour being sold by a client each week to get money for shows; "maid service" being supplied for months to a young mother until she herself laughed about it; meat being distributed to a line of clients when nonrelief families could not afford it. The "babying" of clients, their trickery without detection, and stories of refused private employment were cited in support of the unanimous condemnation of WPA by the town and country, "although it started out with a good purpose." The real failure was that of lack of consistency between WPA and local work and relief values.

The August, 1939, welfare load for the county was 377 cases, 205 of these being in south Hardin. Of these, forty-one cases were from farm background before they went on relief. This, in a county in which almost half of the population lives on farms, shows the relative stability of the farm and town economies in a time of economic stress. The forty-one cases were handled as follows: twenty-eight by WPA; two, widow's pensions; seven, direct relief (four, unemployment; three, ill health); two, medical cases (both confinements);[17] two, care of children. The following analysis is based on the forty-one cases which throw light on the farm picture. The ages of the men on relief range from twenty-one to sixty-six years. The cases are roughly distributed in trimodal fashion; one age group from twenty-five to thirty-

[17] The average number of children for the available small sample with completed families was 6.8, and one woman had borne seventeen children. The welfare department suggested sterilization for those who inquired about birth control.

three, the next forty-one to fifty-one, and the last sixty-two to sixty-six. These include all but five cases. The oldest age group represents men too old to be self-supporting; the middle age group those who entered farm work during the boom and who were forced out by competing younger men; and the youngest age group those who came of age during the depression to find severely limited opportunities both in the country and the city.

The fourteen youngest men (through thirty-seven years) had never been anything but farm laborers. Of the four oldest men, however, two had been share tenants, one a renter, and only one a farm laborer.[18] Between the two extremes of age one finds both types of background, with farm labor becoming more and more dominant among the younger men. This illustrates not only that the farm laborer is in the marginal economic class and is being displaced, but also that opportunities for becoming tenants are increasingly difficult to find. In studying the social origin of these relief cases other pertinent data were available. Only eleven of the thirty-six cases for which there was information were born in the county.[19] More than four-fifths of the farm laborers on relief originated outside of the county. Among the rural relief clients some have had supplemental jobs to farming: garage and truck work, army enlistment, railroad jobs.

There was a general tendency even among nonrelief farmers to expand a marginal farm economy through doing additional work off of the farm. In 1934 over 15 per cent of the farm operators in the county reported that they had done supplementary work for an average of eighty days apiece. Two-thirds of this work was nonagricultural in character, illustrating that a significant number of farmers have evolved a type of "rurban" life advocated by many planners.

Another form of economic adjustment promulgated by

[18] The background of the men then on relief is as follows: Farm laborer, 22; farm renter, 9; share tenant, 4; farm owner, 3 (17, 6, 6 acres). For the Hardin-born men the figures for these backgrounds are, respectively: 4, 3, 1, 3.

[19] Of the twenty-five other cases, places of birth were as follows: Iowa, 7; Illinois, 2; Indiana, 2; Wisconsin, 2; Missouri, 6; North Carolina, 4; Germany, 2.

agricultural planners has been far wider in scope. New Deal government programs have affected every person in the county. In the five years up to mid-1938 various agencies of the national government had loaned more than four and one-half million dollars to Hardin County farmers and had given them outright almost another two million dollars more. During the same period total federal benefits, both repayable and nonrepayable, which were allotted to the nonrural elements of the county amounted to slightly less than a million dollars.[20]

Did the agricultural program alter or preserve rural culture and how? Were the results those sought by the planners and were there effects of which they were unaware? These are certainly vital questions to be answered as a basis for future planning.

Most of the money loaned to farmers was for the purpose of allowing them to avoid foreclosure and to keep their farms through long term mortgages. One function of the agricultural price-control program was to allow the farmers to reduce these same mortgages. Without outside aid, foreclosures would have been so general that the whole farm ownership and incentive pattern would have radically altered. With the government aid, the top rungs of the "agricultural ladder" were secured. This aspect of the agricultural program was that of stabilizing and supporting the old rural pattern.

The AAA program of the Department of Agriculture tried to introduce some distinctly new ideas into the rural culture, such as "parity payments," "soil conservation," "crop reduction," and "corn sealing."[21] To the administrator these were all part and parcel of a single logical plan. For the local culture into which they were introduced they represented new and distinct culture traits. Each had to fit into the rural ways and values. Where there was conflict, the old ways or the new had to change.

[20] *National Emergency Council, Reports*, 1933–38.
Total benefits to Hardin County, $7,299,117.77.
Total nonrepayable, $2,363,214.04.

[21] Government purchase and storage of corn surpluses.

Farm values were not attuned to crop reductions. The whole farm philosophy since the settlement of Iowa, had been one of production. Every available means of increasing production had been eagerly grasped. A good deal of the prestige of agricultural departments and colleges was due to their contributions to this end. As noted, the farm bureau became aware of the relation between surpluses and low prices and requested legislation. Still, in their thinking, the existence of a surplus was the bad thing, not the production of a surplus. In other words, the market was at fault, not the farmer. It is well known that the individualism of the farmer in competition with other farmers forces him to produce as much as possible. Even after the shift in the emphasis of the Department of Agriculture and the farm bureau from "producing more"to "marketing at a profit," the farmers of Hardin County stepped up their production through the general adoption of hybrid seed corn. Government soil conservation men in the field were basically production technicians and such was their continual approach to the farmer.

The social philosopher may recognize a logical trend from governmental desire to control surpluses to legislation to restrict production, but the latter came as an entirely new idea to the farmer's way of life. The man who says he was "not guilty of killing little pigs"[22] has in mind a real sense of guilt. The act was wrong to him, like theft or cheating. Crop reduction made no real sense to the farmer as a way of life. On request he could mouth the economic reasons which necessitated it, but what he usually talked about was the conflict of this new culture trait with his old values. He experienced the lack of consistency between both conservation and government loan agencies, which urged him to produce, and "the program," which cut down his production. Several years of practicing crop reduction did not change his values or his convictions with respect to proper farming methods.[23]

[22] This refers to the AAA initiated slaughter of suckling pigs to start the hog-production control program.

[23] "Proper" methods have long been opposed to abuse of the land, both in theory and practice.

Why then did the farmers enter the program 95 per cent strong?[24] The reason was to secure the cash payments for crop restriction. Even the acceptance of this money was a decidedly new trait, the integration of which into the culture is interesting. Anthropologists are well aware of the fact that new traits entering a culture are made to conform to existing patterns as much as possible. The culture patterns related to the receipt of money were sharply drawn. One received money for services, goods, or "relief." Fortunately for the culture, the farmer's pride and independence precluded his thinking of the AAA payments as relief.[25] This attitude was strengthened, as conditions improved, by the fact that he could really get along without the check. The farmer accepted the money in payment for the crops he could have produced with little additional effort,[26] and for the soil-building procedures he was asked to perform. These were only slight variations of the "goods and services" idea. The idea that the conservation checks were a "parity payment" designed to pay him full measure for what he has produced was foreign to the culture and had made no inroads into it. As a result, the farmer participated in and supported the program because he could make more money thereby. The local patterns and values were unaltered, except for the results of the flow of money. The basic concepts of the planners of the program were either not known or not accepted.

The story was somewhat the same for the "grain sealing" program. The payments for "sealing" corn were accepted in the context of "selling the corn to the government." The latter agency was felt to function as a sort of speculator in corn. The only new aspect was that any eventual profit, over the "sealing" or selling price, would accrue to the farmer. He was aware of this, but doubted that the government would get its original

[24] The 1939 figure for Hardin County. Most nonparticipants tilled such small acreages as to make participation unprofitable.

[25] The farmer considered WPA a form of relief, and the town man considered parity-payment checks to the farmer as relief, but this was simply part of the old rural-urban competition and conflict pattern.

[26] Or as a sort of receipt on "crop insurance," as one farmer put it.

price out of the stored corn. The earlier scheme by which the "government bought corn at around fifty cents and turned around and sold it back to the farmer for around thirty, without the corn even leaving the bins," simply made the government out to be "silly." The later plan was far preferable, but again there was lack of conviction or even understanding of the "normal" cycle of good and poor crop years which was basic to the "sealing" program. In 1939 when "resealing" allowances caused a great expansion of bin building on the farms, lack of belief in the permanency of the system found concrete expression in the fact that of the one hundred and twenty bins built by the largest contractor not a single one was built for that purpose alone. They were all constructed to be converted into brooder houses, garages, tenant houses, pig pens, etc. This lack of understanding of the planners' idea was not due to a dearth of educational meetings, which were numerous and well attended. It was due to lack of conformity of these ideas with the established culture. On the whole, the "corn sealing" program made more sense to the farmer than crop reductions did, for the former was more consistent with his ways of life. No relation was felt to exist between the two programs.

The soil conservation work was very popular. It simply furthered values already extant in the county—increased production and proper care of the soil. The technical adviser's position resembled that of the county agent. The county representative of the Soil Conservation Service (SCS) himself stated that the same results now obtained through "contracts" and Civilian Conservation Corps work could be had by simply sending technical advisers into the field. Farmers were quick to apply to their own farms methods which they saw in practice in farms operated under conservation-contract with the government. This was one aspect of the agricultural program which would have been continued even without government subsidy. As Hardin County had no real problem of soil erosion, this justification of crop control was rather thin. Actually, conservation men advised farmers to "mine your soil when prices are high," the thing which has always been done.

The Rural Electrification Administration (REA) played into a real cultural need and met with great success. The lines were first energized in 1937, and there were 745 consumers in December, 1939.[27] The manager expected to have another four hundred customers. Private utilities had abused the farmer until they were heartily disliked. As soon as confidence in the new co-operative was founded, its low rates made possible long desired electrification.[28] The new electric lines made possible the acquisition of a wide variety of electrical equipment. This was consistent with the rural desire to make the farm home like that of the city. Estimates based on a questionnaire circulated by REA and the county agent showed the cost of new electrical equipment to equal three-fourths of the cost of the new lines themselves.[29] Securing electricity was practically synonymous with getting a new radio, a washing machine, and an electric iron.[30] One-third of the new customers also bought refrigerators, vacuum cleaners, toasters, cream separators, and motors of less than one horsepower. These items were almost entirely conveniences which could not be expected to pay for themselves or their operation.

The Farm Security Administration tenant purchase plan became operative in the county with the purchase of four farms in 1939. So careful was the selection of the tenants that it was the opinion of the county agent and others that most of the young men would have eventually climbed the agricultural ladder and bought farms without assistance.

The county planning board of Hardin County was selected by the president of the farm bureau and represented a real attempt to get the cross section of the county necessary to any worth-while planning. Its worst fault was overweighting with

[27] This included seven townships in neighboring counties.

[28] It must be remembered that in this area of high standards of living, electricity constitutes a cultural need to a far greater extent than in other areas.

[29] Lines, $329,000; equipment estimate, $245,000.

[30] Iron, 92 per cent of the consumers; washing machine, 81 per cent; radio, 80 per cent.

nontenants and local AAA functionaries.[31] This was particularly striking as the problem chosen for consideration in 1940 was tenant-owner relationships. To judge solely on the basis of a single meeting of the board, its efficacy was to be doubted. Two extension agents from out of the county dominated the meeting, and the members were dubious as to what problems to consider, and even more uncertain as to the ultimate value of anything they could accomplish.

This resumé of the type of integration achieved between the New Deal farm programs and the local culture leads one to the specific reactions of the people of the county to those plans. There was apparently considerable resistance among the farmers to the first agricultural programs, due both to suspicion and to a real dislike for being told how to run their farms. "Regimentation" was on many lips and was full of adverse emotional connotation. However, an unsatisfactory culture is ripe for change. Farmers grasped at any government plan which offered salvation from their economic difficulties just as they evolved movements of their own to better conditions. The fact that the word "regimentation" had fallen from usage by 1939 indicated some acceptance of the new ways. This was probably a result of the integration of old values and the new program in the manner discussed above.

The local newspaper is more urban than rural in its attitude, but even its limited influence on farm readers makes its content noteworthy. During the early years of the New Deal the paper devoted a great amount of space and enthusiasm to the agricultural programs. When the "need for explanation" was past, it became editorial policy to devote less space to the AAA. This was not as significant as a noticeable change in attitude. The paper did not attack the program outright but through innuendo in the editorials. In an issue giving front-page headlines

[31] On the board were seven owner-operators, four tenant-relatives, two tenants, a farm manager, a nonoperating owner, the SCS representative, and the county agent. These included the county AAA chairman, four township chairmen, one township committeeman, a county corn sealer, a man not in the AAA program, and one man who was strongly Republican.

to the hundreds of thousands of dollars coming into the county through conservation payments, an editorial on California's "ham and eggs" plan concluded: "There is one sticker in all of these schemes. There are certain great economic laws which no state or nation has power to repeal. One of these is that wealth is made by producing and not by spending." In another instance, an editorial in this Democratic paper states: "Kansas wheat growers and farm experts find indications that the soil conservation activities of the farm program may nullify crop control efforts made by way of acreage reduction. . . . But this is not a cause for unfavorable criticism of the soil program." Another section, commenting on the improved indices of farm conditions, concluded: "Parity payments and other AAA measures also enter into the picture. But the farmers would prefer, and properly so, that this difference in the index prices of what they have to buy and the products they sell be equalized directly rather than to have some part of the discrepancy made up by government checks."

The results of an opinion poll conducted in the county on agricultural problems and programs illustrate some sharp differences of opinion, which correlate with the social elements expressing them.[32] The informants could be divided on the basis of the questionnaire data into businessmen and farmers. The farmer group was subdivided on the basis of type of farm operator and size of farm. The greatest difference of opinion existed between farmers and businessmen. The former said that soil conservation was a national problem, with which only one businessman agreed. No business people indicated that the "farmers had a poorer living than most other people," whereas a number of the farmers thought so. Half of the businessmen

[32] A copy of the questionnaire and the tabulated responses for Iowa is to be found in Roland Welborn and Herbert G. Folken, "Land and Man," *Iowa Farm Econ.*, October, 1939. The Hardin sample is small, only fifty-seven blanks in all, but in spite of this it illustrates the manner in which an "opinionnaire" can be utilized to confirm and elaborate a cultural analysis of modern society.

said the AAA was "undue governmental interference with Iowa farmers," but practially no farmers agreed. Rural-urban competition is obvious in these differences in response.

The same tendency for opinions to reflect group values is to be found among various types of farmers. Tenants all felt a need for "state farm tenancy legislation"; owners and tenant-relatives agreed to a lesser extent, particularly the tenant-relatives, who are neither real tenants nor owners. The owners of large farms were divided on the question of the advisability of reducing the number of farmers, but small owners and all tenants were against it to a man. Of course, large owners were more convinced than were small owners that farming does not provide a poorer living.

Interviews with a drug clerk, a clothing-store operator, and a meat-market owner in Eldora produced material in conformity with the results of the questionnaire. All felt that the agricultural program was a relief measure which had run too long. They felt concern over the large national debt, which did not perturb the farmer. Along the main street of Iowa Falls, the New Deal had only one supporter. Farm attitude toward the New Deal was generally doubtful or adverse, with the exception of the farm program.[33] In its voting behavior in the 1938 national and state elections, the county was almost evenly divided between Democrats and Republicans. The towns had Republican majorities in contrast to the rural areas.[34]

A most striking example of cultural patterning of the reaction of a group to an innovation is to be seen in the attitude of

[33] The general tenor of farm attitude toward the New Deal was apparently well evaluated. In the 1940 presidential election, a year after this study was made, Hardin County went Republican, 5,692 to 4,764. Twelve of the nineteen precincts gave Republican majorities in 1940 and again in 1944. The total vote in 1944 was 5,059 Republican to 3,975 Democratic.

[34] In the Nov. 8, 1938, general election the county vote was: for senator, 3,279 Republican, 3,448 Democratic; for governor, 3,492 Republican, 3,279 Democratic. Of the seven precincts giving Republican majorities, five were towns. Eldora gave a majority of 156 and Iowa Falls one of 185. County politics is still basically Republican. Eleven out of twelve county officials were Republican in 1939.

the small-town businessmen toward the farm programs. They identified their interests with those of "big business" and industry. They conceived of the farmers as being dependent upon them for goods and services. Their own dependence upon the farmers was minimized. Only by understanding this cultural pattern can one comprehend the townsman's antagonism to a government program, which had poured millions of dollars into the small trade centers through increasing the income of the farmers.

The cultural description here concluded has tried to present the broad picture of a dynamic modern farm society and its reaction to attempts to create social change. The local culture is selective in its acceptance of innovations. Each new culture trait is interpreted in terms of the local culture. For a trait to be accepted, it must not seriously conflict with the culture. Crop production is not a simple cultural element, to be seen only in relation to demand and the price structure. Crop restriction conflicts with the basic rural philosophy of maximum production. Nor is this philosophy just an economic one. It pervades the rural evaluations of men's status and even their character. In such a culture, payments to farmers to restrict their productive acreages will not change their philosophy of life.

Directed social change is not easily achieved. The most important tools at the disposal of social planners are the social sciences. The tendency of some administrators to think of these tools as instruments "to fit the people to the plan" runs counter to the fact that culture itself is the limiting factor in social change. The plan is the adaptable element. The proper role of the social scientist is to provide insight through which planning can be adapted to the society in question It is unlikely that major policy decisions will, or even should, be made by social scientists. It would appear that their role in the implementation of determined policy should be an increasing one.

REFERENCES

BEE, LAWRENCE. The Incidence of Selected Social Factors Upon Old Age Dependency. Unpublished master's thesis, Iowa State College, 1937.

BELL, EARL H. In the Wilderness, A Study of Contemporary Life. Unpublished doctoral dissertation, Univ. Wisconsin, 1931.

BENTON, T. H., and W. W. STRIKE. Soil Survey of Hardin County, Iowa. Washington: U. S. Dept. Agric., 1923.

CLAMPITT, FRANK T. Some Incidents in My Life. Ann Arbor, Mich., 1935.

Consumers Market Data Handbook, 1939.

CURTISS, C. F. The Population of Iowa, Its Composition and Changes. Ames: Iowa State College, 1930.

Eldora Herald.

Eldora Herald-Ledger.

GALPIN, C. J., and T. B. MANNY. Interstate Migration. Washington: Dept. Agric., 1934.

History of Hardin County. Springfield, Ill.: Union Publ. Co., 1883.

HOLMES, C. L., and C. W. CRICKMAN. Types of Farming in Iowa, II. Ames: Iowa State College, 1938.

MANGUS, A. R. Cultural Regions within the Rural-Farm Population. Washington: Div. Soc. Res., Works Progress Administration, 1938.

National Emergency Council, Reports. Washington, D. C., 1936–39.

QUICK, HERBERT. Vandemark's Folly. Indianapolis: Bobbs-Merrill, 1922.

SIMMONS, DOROTHY. Family Living Expenditure of 160 Farm Families in 1938. Ames: Iowa State College.

SOTH, LAUREN K. Agricultural Economic Facts, Basebook of Iowa. Ames: Iowa State College, 1936.

STEVENSON, W. H., and P. E. BROWN. Soil Survey of Iowa, Hardin County. Ames: Iowa State College, 1925.

STONG, PHIL. State Fair. New York: Grosset and Dunlap, 1933.

SUCKOW, RUTH. The Folks. New York: Farrar and Rinehart, 1934.

SUMMERS, H. B. The Iowa Radio Audience, 1939. 2d ed.; Manhattan: Kansas State College, 1939.

TAYLOR, CARL C., and others. Disadvantage Classes in American Agriculture. U. S. Dept. Agric., Soc. Res. Rept., No. VIII, April, 1928.

U. S. Department of Commerce. Religious Bodies, 1926. Washington, 1930. Vol. I.

U. S. Census of Agriculture, 1935. Washington, 1936.

U. S. Sixteenth Census of the U. S., 1940. Washington, 1942-43. Vols. I, II.

WAKELEY, RAY E. Differential Mobility within the Rural Population in 18 Iowa Townships, 1928 to 1935. Ames: Iowa State College, 1938.

WELBORN, ROLAND, and HERBERT G. FOLKEN. Land and Man. Iowa Farm Economist, October, 1939.

www.ingramcontent.com/pod-product-compliance
Lightning Source LLC
LaVergne TN
LVHW050022250826
846302LV00008B/61